D1549976

My Secret World

Also by Pauline Kidner:

Life with Bluebell

My Secret World

Pauline Kidner

BCA

LONDON   NEW YORK   SYDNEY   TORONTO

This edition published 1995 by BCA
by arrangement with Robinson Publishing Ltd
CN 9839

Copyright © Pauline Kidner 1995

Illustrations by Jason Venus

Photography: *first colour section* Jason Venus, John
Roberts, author, author, Jason Venus, author, author,
author, Jason Venus, Richard Austin, Mike Hollist, author;
b/w section Ken Chapman, Ken Chapman, Ken Chapman,
Ken Chapman, Ken Chapman, Ken Chapman, Richard
Austin, Richard Austin, Richard Austin, Ken Chapman,
Ken Chapman, Ken Chapman, Ken Chapman; *second
colour section* Robert Dunstan, author, Vanessa Latford,
Jason Venus, John Roberts, Jason Venus, author, Mike
Hollist, Johanne de Meeste.

Printed and bound in the EC

Contents

Dedicated with love to my Mum and Dad, Eddie and Joy Masterson

Can I borrow . . . ?, Is it alright if . . . ?, Would you mind doing . . . ?, Do you think you could . . . ?

The answer has always been – Yes. Thank you to both of you, for everything – you're the best.

Introduction

Sarah Kennedy and I were standing in the middle of a field near Cheddar Gorge. At our feet was a small, covered cage. Pauline crouched down and opened the door of the cage. Nothing happened. We all stood and waited. Then, suddenly, a startled brown form with enormous ears emerged and scampered a short distance away. It stopped briefly and looked around it, seeing for the first time in its life a vast space spreading out in all directions. With only a momentary pause it was gone, racing across the field towards the long grasses at its far edge. There it disappeared and we all relaxed. It was another triumph for a woman who has selflessly devoted herself to caring for animals of many kinds, year after year.

The little animal in question was not a precious rarity. It was only a brown hare, and yet to Pauline it was just as important as any giant panda or Bengal tiger. It had been brought to her, near death, as a tiny leveret and she had nursed it and nurtured it, feeding it every hour on the hour, both day and night, until it could be weaned. A long, uninterrupted night's sleep is something of a luxury for Pauline.

Then, under her protective gaze, she saw the leveret slowly turn into a hare, growing strong and healthy, until it was ready to be returned to the wild. She chose the release spot carefully, searching for a place where there were no enemies to exploit its naivety in the wild.

She watched it go with mixed emotions, like a parent watching a child leave home. She was sad for herself but happy for the hare and for the chance she had given it, against all the odds.

Introduction

Sarah and I were not surprised when David Bellamy and Lee Durrell, our judges for the 'Animal Country' Award, chose Pauline Kidner as the 1995 winner from a list of excellent finalists. And it was a great pleasure for us to return to Pauline's animal centre, that she calls her 'Secret World', to surprise her with the award and congratulate her for all the wonderful things she has been doing, both in her work to rescue and rehabilitate animals that find themselves in trouble and, equally importantly, in her efforts to educate the public concerning the need to protect wildlife and the ways in which this can be done.

Pauline is an example of that special kind of human being who thinks far more about the animals in her care than she does about herself. A less self-centred person it would be hard to find. And yet through all the problems she faces, she manages to retain a cheerfulness and a buoyant pleasure in what she herself is learning from the animals, week after week.

Her task is never-ending. Sadly there will always be more and more animals finding themselves in trouble that will need the assistance that her centre offers. One can only hope that she, and others like her, will always be there to offer them an expert, helping hand.

It gives me great pleasure to welcome you to her world through the pages of this book and to share with her some of the challenging involvements she encounters. And when you have read it, take a day out to visit her 'Secret World' and see for yourself what she is doing. You will, I am sure, be as impressed as Sarah and I were, when we took our Animal Country cameras there not so long ago to show as wide an audience as possible her splendid work. Long may she continue.

Desmond Morris

1

Saturday's Child

There are not many nights that I don't wander out to the front of our farm, where the barn door entrance is lit displaying the name 'Secret World: Badger and Wildlife Rescue Centre'. This is a special place to me, for I sit by a flower bed in memory of an animal. Odd to be out in the dark, you may say, but then darkness was the time that we shared. She was really the start of all my wildlife work and the reason for it now – I miss her.

From an early age, in a very happy childhood, my love of animals was nurtured by being 'allowed' to have pets to enjoy, although, if the truth be known, my mother's love of animals had a great deal to do with it. At school, I can remember proudly reciting the list of pets that we had – three dogs, one rabbit, a guinea pig, two goldfish, a hamster and two budgies.

My sister and I were taught to respect animals and appreciate their needs as well as our 'wants' – anyone who has pushed a dressed-up dog in a doll's pram will know what I mean! Feeding time was always punctual, as our meals were for us; and even then I realized how animals respond to routine and conversation.

Hammy the hamster, complete with cage, was kept in the kitchen. (This was well before environmental health became a big concern!) He found it dreadfully hard, being a nocturnal creature, to drag himself out of bed for his small portion of the porridge that was cooked on cold winter mornings, but drag himself out he did as soon as the smell wafted from the cooker. The bleary-eyed face pushed its sensitive nose to the bars, keen to make everyone aware that he had managed to get up and to make sure he did not get forgotten.

We unfortunately had quite a few hamsters in our younger years, partly due to the shortness of their natural life but also due to the fact that my sister June did not like to have a bath on her own – she was only 10 at the time. Of course, when one is scared of the dark in a big house, it is understandable that the company of a hamster running round the bathroom floor, whilst you are bathing, gives one the confidence to be in the bathroom alone. A careless evacuation of the bath without scanning the floor first caused the demise of our first Hammy – despite the administration of brandy, which was mother's sure-fire 'survive or die' treatment, and which, I must admit, did at times work.

Hammy 2's demise was even more tragic; our bathroom door was one of those that you had to slam to get it to shut, and yes – you've guessed, at least it was quick death. Hammy 3 was luckier as by this time June had outgrown the need for company in the bathroom and he led a full and happy life. We did lose him on one occasion, though, when we had had him out in our dolls' house and suddenly realized he was gone. A full search followed, with many tears and accusations as to who should have been watching him. Sadly, after about an hour we had to admit defeat and just hope he would turn up on his own. The whole family, Dad, Mum, June and I, were sitting watching television in the evening when my mother started to laugh and pointed to the top of the settee. A lump under the loose covers of the settee was propelling its way down to the cushions – Hammy 3 had returned!

Our budgies commandeered the nest boxes provided and bred some young; the guinea-pig was allowed to have babies and one of our corgis had puppies, so I was soon conversant with the joys of looking after tiny animals – the clearing up (although Mum did most of that!) and the sadness when it's time for the youngsters to

2

go to new homes, and you so hope that they will be cared for and loved. Pets must be given time and company. I have been lucky that I seem to have an affinity with mammals, and have been accused of caring more for animals than for humans at times – I make no comment!

This is probably the reason for the ruination of my debut on the stage at the age of 8, in our Sunday School concert. To add interest to my recital of 'Run Rabbit Run', it was arranged for me to hold our pet rabbit. In the first performance, she sat so quietly in my arms that no one realized she was real so, in order to instigate some movement, I was despatched to the side of the stage for the second performance complete with lettuce leaf in my pocket to 'obtain action'. Nerves being what they are, I was unaware that this lettuce leaf was deftly lifted from my pocket and eaten whilst I waited my turn, only to find that the bait was missing once I got on stage and the rotten rabbit remained totally still for the second performance too. Maybe this was to be my very first lesson in working with animals and photography, but more of that later.

We moved several times through my childhood as Dad, a policeman in the Kent constabulary, was promoted, but no matter where we were, we were always able to find nearby country walks to take the dogs. My father always did the morning walk and the afternoon walk was shared by Mum, June and myself. The first walks I can really remember were when we lived at Walderslade and opposite our house was an unmade road leading to the woods.

Even then, autumn was my favourite season. We lived in aptly named Chestnut Avenue, where the street was lined with sweet chestnut trees; many a return journey from school was spent wading through the mounds of golden leaves that had fallen into the gutter, kicking them high and watching them somersault down the road as the wind seemed to bring them to life. And if it was raining, that really made my day. Rivulets of water cascaded down the road, glistening beneath the street lamps as the day was already drawing in. Lights would shine from the houses with windows steamed up by the warmth. Wrapped up with hat and scarf, cheeks glowing from the exertion of wading through all the leaves, I hoped that a hot drink would be ready once I got home – and maybe even crumpets! How vivid memories can be.

Walking in the woods with the dogs, I was very unaware of the wildlife, as I am sure many other young people are. We just accept that it is there. I was fascinated by the array of fungi and moss found clinging to fallen trees, not realizing it was all part of the life-cycle as they slowly cause the decomposition of dead and dying leaf litter and wood, creating nutrients to rejuvenate the soil ready for the explosion of the new generation of plants to grow in the spring. It never occurred to me that the countryside consisted of habitats and species, nor that it needed protecting; hopefully education is now making more people aware.

When we moved to Willesborough, near Ashford, our walks took us through more open fields and up to Hinxhill Farm. On walking the dogs up to the farm one day, I came across a sight I was not expecting. It was to be my first experience of seeing a gamekeeper's trophy fence where what he considered to be vermin he had caught and hung up on barbed wire to show that he is doing his job. Moles, squirrels, stoats and weasels hung in macabre array. Nowadays these things are not commonplace. Happily, the reduction of gamekeepers since the Second World War has allowed many species to recover in numbers, such as the polecat, which surely would have become extinct in this country if persecution had continued.

I hurried on past this spectacle and got into the habit of always looking the other way once I got to this part of the walk. Beyond, up a steep hill, was the farm that I visited. It was a large dairy farm and I was allowed to go and look at the milk calves, some still very young and keen to suck your fingers, and see the impressive Hereford bull, with the shiny copper ring through his nose. I loved the sweet smell of hay and the pungent aroma of the cowstalls. An hour could slip by quite quickly just mooching around, but it never occurred to me that farming would interest me as a career in later life.

Once into my teenage years, I managed to get a summer job giving donkey rides on the beach at Dymchurch. We used to collect the donkeys from St Mary's Bay and ride them down to the beach. Long sunny days were spent walking up and down with the donkeys, and wet days were spent in the arcades waiting for the rain to stop. These were happy days of jukeboxes, candyfloss and beach illuminations, which consisted of a few coloured lights strung on a sagging black wire near the entrance to the sandy beach.

My donkey Bambi was a lovely cream colour and we became pals. She even came to us during the winter as Dad rented a field for us. She was a very clever donkey and had a wonderful trick

– when she was eating plums, she could spit the stone out, which I thought was very clever.

Dymchurch was to be the place for my first true love. Not that I can remember much about it, other than his name was James and he helped with the donkeys as well. I really must have been keen because the one thing I can remember was that he always had cheese and onion sandwiches for his lunch and it made his breath smell. It was probably why the 'love' did not last very long!

It came as quite a shock when, after 27 years' service, my father decided to retire from the police force and take up an appointment as Managing Clerk to the Clerk of the Peace in Bristol. This meant that we moved to Somerset. My sister at this time was already working on a farm at High Halden. She stayed behind in Kent and has remained there ever since, having married and raised a family.

When we moved to Somerset, I loved it. Here was a different kind of countryside. Gone were the fruit orchards of Kent, the conical roofs of the oasthouses that dried the hops, and the chalk Downs. Here was a richer, wetter scenery with one of the largest varieties of bird and animal life.

My first priority had to be to look for a job. Having refused to return to school at 15 (my mother's obstinate streak in me!) I had no qualifications, and my first try at shop work failed miserably. After only three weeks, I just knew that this was not the life for me.

It was Dad who suggested that I looked at a job in farming and soon I was on my way for an interview for a job as a dairymaid at a farm near Thornbury. Pennywell Farm was run by a Mr and Mrs Ball who had a herd of Guernsey and Jersey cows; they also kept deep litter poultry. With the job came a caravan which was a little way from the farmhouse, but meals were provided and my washing was done for me, so I was absolutely thrilled when I was offered the job.

The farm was down a winding lane, away from the village, and we had no neighbours apart from an elderly couple who lived at the end of the road. Unpacking my things in my very own caravan away from home at the age of 15, it was all a very big step.

'Saturday's child works hard for a living', they say: and this Saturday baby was about to find out that this was so! My day started at 6 a.m. and finished at 6 p.m. I worked for 12 days and then had a weekend off, but on the weekend that I worked, I only had to do the milking and see to the chickens so there was time in the middle of the day to relax.

Rising at 5.30 a.m. to be ready for 6, I was soon shown how to bring the cows in for milking. I had gone into farming at the right time of year – it was August and even the early mornings were warm. Taking the farm bike, I would cycle up the lane. There were several copses between the fields and the air would be full of bird-song. When I reached the field I would lean the bike against a tree, and open the large wooden gate which needed to be swung back against the hedge. Then, walking out into the field, I would call the cows, most of them still lying chewing their cud. Slowly and awkwardly, they would rise, some taking their time, others running shaking their heads with excitement. The Jerseys, with their pretty black faces and huge eyes, looked almost deer-like with their spindly legs. The Guernsey cows were a redder colour with white patches, although they all varied in their markings and their size.

Counting them as they passed me out on to the lane, I noticed that even at this time of the morning a haze of midge flies hovered over them as they made their way down the lane towards the milking parlour. With tails swishing, the cows ambled down the lane and I followed on the bike.

As we neared the farm I would ride through them, just to make sure that they turned in at the gate, but they knew where they were going. Even the ones that would ignore the gate, and walk up to me and sniff with their large wet black noses, were only being inquisitive; they would soon draw back and jaunt away, joining the quieter ones on the way to the shed.

The farmhouse was fairly old but Mr and Mrs Ball had done quite a lot of building work and it was all in good order. The large outbuildings surrounded the yard and a stone staircase led to a storage room at the top of the stone barn. It was from the top of the staircase that we often saw the Berkeley Hunt pass through in all their regalia; more often than not, about ten minutes later you would see the fox retracing his steps, having doubled back on the hounds.

To start with, the cows were milked in the large cowshed, tied up by their necks. It was my job to wash their udders before Mr Ball came along behind with the milking pails and put the clusters on. This was the only time I had the chance to learn their names, and many I began to know from the back end first – it took a lot longer to recognize them by their faces.

Eventually a new parlour was installed and I was able to milk on my own. I learnt so much while I was there. Both the Jersey and the Guernsey cows give very rich creamy milk. They all had different temperaments: there were those that wanted to be milked first and others who preferred to be last, or those that wanted to stand in a left-hand stall rather than a right-hand stall. Each cow was individual; even now I can remember Katie, a tubby Guernsey cow who hated me and kicked if ever she got the chance!

I experienced seeing calves being born, usually at night. What effort and hard work, after nine months of pregnancy, the cow has to go through for that final moment as the wet, steaming calf slips into its new world. Lying on the ground, it summons the strength to lift its head and snorts the birth fluids from its nose. Then, shaking its head, it peers around through enormous eyelashes. Within minutes, the calf is shakily scrabbling to its feet. The cow licks it to stimulate the heart and to dry the wet skin. Gently mooing, she bonds with it as her own so that even when the cow is put back with the herd, she will recognize her own calf, and it will know her.

A cow has her first calf when she is approximately three years old; she is still known as a heifer until she has her second calf, as it is not until then that she will peak in her milk production.

As with all mammals, in the first 48 hours after the cow has given birth she produces colostrum, a thick, special milk that contains many antibodies. If any young mammal does not receive this they are unlikely to survive. After the first two days her milk will return to normal, and then what milk remains after the calf has drunk his fill can be added to the tank for human consumption. A cow has to have a calf every year in order to produce milk. She will have a calf and be in milk for ten months, then she will be 'dried off' as by that time her milk yield will have decreased. Then she will join the other dry cows and have a resting period for two months before calving again ready for her next lactation.

Feeding, cleaning and moving the cows all takes a lot of time. With the morning milking over, and the cows back in the fields, it would now be round about 9 a.m. – breakfast time, and by now you were more than ready for cereals, egg and bacon.

Starting again at 10 a.m., it was time to see to the chickens:

feed them, check their water and collect the eggs. With the deep litter system, the hens had a large area for perching, an area full of shavings for exercise and nesting boxes all around the sides of the houses. Bags of meal had to be carried on your shoulder, in order to fill the food troughs. A lot of it was heavy, hard work but I thoroughly enjoyed it.

The best part of keeping chickens was that we reared them from one day old. Once the house was all cleaned out ready for them, the chicks would arrive in cardboard boxes. Pretty little fluffy chicks were placed in the house with infra-red lamps glowing to keep them warm. Given their freedom, after travelling in the boxes, they would dart around on the shavings, cheeping and keeping constantly on the move searching for food; then, as with all young things, they would tire. One by one, they would lie down beside each other under the lamps until a carpet of yellow fluff covered the sawdust floor and the odd sleepy eye opened and then closed again.

As with all things, when dealing with animals there will be highs and lows. I loved the summer, the animals, the new births, loves made all the sweeter by contrast when things would go wrong. The sorrow and sadness when the slippery form falls from the cow and remains silent and still – to watch a cow nudge the new-born calf, gently lowing, not understanding why her stillborn calf is not moving. The disasters that occur when electricity fails and those lovely fluffy chicks are found crowded and dead from the cold. The times when the vet makes it clear that an animal with mastitis or milk fever is not going to make it, and the natural culling that is necessary in farming when an animal reaches its final day of maturity or usefulness on the farm.

Unless you have been involved in farming and really understand the logistics, the caring, the way of life that the farming community carries on it is impossible to form an opinion on this subject. There are many things that I do not like about farming but I understand the reasons for them. People have lived in this lifestyle for hundreds of years, living hand to mouth – closer to nature you cannot get. Human numbers, greed, supply and demand have got us to where we are now – it's called progress. Living on the farm then, I don't suppose I even thought about the issues that are discussed these days. It was a way of life and you accepted it.

It wasn't so easy to accept the cold! Winter came, and although I do enjoy the winter with its frosty mornings and misty days, having to break ice on water troughs and chipping away at frozen dung brought a whole new meaning to it. My caravan was really cold, and when I had been away for the weekend my bedclothes would stand up where they were, damp and frozen! It took a good hour to warm the place up again. My hands were the worst thing as they became very sore, and when I woke in the morning they would bleed as I tried to flex them.

The saving grace was the porridge at breakfast time, sprinkled with brown sugar and fresh yellow cream skimmed from the churn. Still, the winter didn't kill me and I'd do it again!

Soon after I went to Pennywell, I was given a young puppy. It was the first dog that had really been my own. I called her Penny after all the puddles she produced, but she was gorgeous. Black and tan, she was a real mixture, but she was very loyal and followed me everywhere. Penny was company for me in the caravan too. She would sleep at the foot of my bed (extra heating) but was up ready to go as soon as it was time to fetch the cows. By the time she had been with me four months we had built up a routine. Most of the time she was with me, but occasionally she would wander off, though never too far.

It was one Sunday afternoon and I had been listening to the radio in the caravan when I heard her coming. I hadn't really realized she had been missing until then as she had walked over with me after lunch and then stayed by the doorstep. Her sides were heaving and she began to retch. Immediately, I realized she was going to be sick, so I quickly picked her up and carried her outside. As I placed her on the ground, her legs gave way and she began to vomit. Watching, I began to see that there was something seriously wrong. Her body began to tremble. Running quickly, I called to Mr Ball who came to see what was wrong. By now Penny was frothing at the mouth. Quickly contacting the vet, Mr Ball offered to drive me in. The journey seemed to take ages. By now Penny was having spasms, her eyes were rolling, and saliva drooled from her mouth. She was unconscious. I began to realize the journey was not going to save her.

I gently carried her in to the vet but she was dying before my eyes. Even as I placed her on the table, it was obvious that there was nothing the vet could do. With a terrible moan, and a horrible gurgling sound rattling in her throat, her body went completely stiff and she collapsed dead.

Tears streamed down my face. I couldn't believe that only an hour ago she had been with me, fit and healthy, and now she lay dead with her face tortured in pain. The vet explained that she showed classic symptoms of strychnine poison, which she could well have picked up from a poisoned carcass which farmers sometimes leave around for foxes. I could not comprehend how anyone could deliberately try to kill any animal by these grotesque means. Penny must have wandered on to some adjoining land to have picked it up. But I never had another dog while at Pennywell Farm, it was too risky.

My social life began when I joined the Young Farmers Club – it must be one of the best dating agencies ever. We had a lot of fun with meetings every week that always ended up in the pub, hockey on Bristol Downs, dances, competitions, the lot. On the nights I did not go out, I would be in bed by 7.30 p.m. to try and catch up on my sleep!

It was Christmastime, and the young farmers all went round carol-singing to various houses, wishing people Merry Christmas and collecting for charity. Many of the houses expected us and laid on treats for us to eat. It was a cold evening, but we were wrapped up warmly, and it was fun to join in the festive spirit.

I'm afraid I started the evening with one young farmer and came home with another! Jimmy was to become my husband. We went out for over a year before finally marrying. Jimmy was the oldest son of Mr and Mrs Nichols who farmed at Pool Farm near Thornbury. They had a large Friesian herd and I spent weekends there helping Jimmy and getting to know the family.

I was accepted into the family, and it was a large one too. When I first visited the farm to meet everyone, I noticed how different the farm was from where I worked; it was much bigger, and they had pigs as well as cows and chickens. The large, roomy farmhouse had a huge kitchen with a lovely Aga to warm by. Mrs Nichols did all her cooking on the Aga and Sunday was always the day that the family sat down together. Jimmy had three brothers and a sister: Brian was 19, Elisabeth 11, Derek was 8 and Tommy was 4. It seemed funny to be part of a big family.

Mrs Nichols had the ability to supply inexhaustible meals and anyone, if they called in around mealtimes, was always asked to stay, whether it be the paper man or a feed rep. (This did cause problems when Jimmy thought I could do the same, and we ended up with three people sitting round two chops!)

One of the local characters was Ern, a very elderly man who

lived on his own and delivered the newspapers. He always wore a long trenchcoat-type mac, tied at the waist with a piece of string, and an old pair of baggy trousers. His outfit was finished off with a pair of shiny black dancing shoes. The small amount of hair that he had stood up in wisps, and he smiled a lot despite the fact that he only had two teeth – one on the top and one on the bottom. Jimmy would tease Ern mercilessly about his teeth.

'Only got two teeth, haven't you Ern', he would say.

'Ahrr,' said Ern, winking – he knew what was coming from the ritual they went through every visit.

'A chopper and a chewer, in'it, Ern', Jimmy joked and they both laughed together.

Ern was very much a man of habit. He always delivered his papers at the same time every day, covering the same route. He lived further down in the village and the road that he travelled was crossed by the new road leading to Oldbury Power Station. As the amount of traffic built up over a period of time, a set of traffic lights was erected at the crossroads.

It was only a week later that an unfortunate man on his way to work at the power station, seeing the green lights ahead, did not slow down. Much to his horror, Ernie sailed straight out on his bicycle and it was impossible for the car to avoid him. Ern was injured but luckily not killed. Both the police and the ambulance were called.

On trying to find out the details of the accident the policeman questioned Ern as to what had happened.

'Oi was on my bike,' Ern explained, 'when this silly man came flying down the road and ran me over. Don't 'e know I d'always come through here at 11.30 each morning?'

'Yes, sir,' replied the police officer, 'but what colour were the traffic lights?' he asked Ern.

'What traffic lights?' was Ern's reply.

Ern recovered from his accident and learnt the Highway Code.

Jimmy and I married when I was 17 and Jimmy was 25. We moved to a farm called Great Leaze, which was just down the road from Pool Farm where Jimmy continued to work. To start with we lived in a caravan but eventually we moved into the old farmhouse at Great Leaze once it had been modernized.

Great Leaze Farm was an old dilapidated place but I loved it,

'What Traffic Lights?'

12

and it had a lovely atmosphere. The old apple orchard was no longer used commercially; its gnarled trees were amazing shapes and in the winter, when the branches were bare, balls of mistletoe could be seen.

I still occasionally see mistletoe as we travel the motorways in the winter, but because it usually grows up in the canopy of the tree, in the summer the leaves hide it. When the seed of the mistletoe germinates, it anchors itself to the tree by putting out tentacles. These penetrate the bark and grow into the tissues of the tree in order to take water and nutrients from the tree's sap. But it is not a complete parasite as, once it has established itself, it grows leaves, and so is able to produce some of its own requirements through photosynthesis.

The mistletoe puts out flowers in April or May but they are very inconspicuous. The flowers are followed by the white berries that we know from the sprays hung above doorways at Christmas. The berries are eaten by birds and some get dispersed through their droppings, but more often than not a sticky substance on the seed causes it to stick to the bill of the bird as it feeds, and it is only later as the bird wipes its beak on another branch to clean it that the seed is transferred. The sticky substance allows the seed to stick to the bark, thus giving it time to germinate.

The Druids used mistletoe – it was given out to hang in people's houses to ward off evil. It was also believed that mistletoe improved fertility, provided it was not allowed to touch the ground – maybe this is where kissing under the mistletoe is derived from!

Family life began with the arrival of my daughter Wendy, quickly followed one year later by another daughter, Kerry. We had many friends who married around the same time, and with all our socializing, our lives were full.

I decided to learn to drive and travelled to Bristol for my lessons. Jimmy did take me for some lessons but we always ended up arguing. I would go to Bristol for my driving lesson and then on to my parents who were then living in Clevedon. I'm glad I learnt to drive in the middle of a city because you certainly do not have any fear of busy places once you have experienced the city centre of Bristol.

I'm afraid I failed my first driving test, and had to take a lot of ribbing from Jimmy, so I did not tell him when I had my second test. This time I passed, and then went straight on to my parents. Jimmy came over to pick me up and made a casual remark about my driving; I did not bother to tell him I had passed my test.

'You'd better drive home', said Jimmy as we left, 'you need the practice.'

I took the keys. As we drove along, I was reminded of what I was doing wrong and quietly seethed. We usually came home by the A38 because, being a learner, I could not use the motorway. But this night, now a qualified driver, I swung on to the motorway.

'You can't go on here!' Jimmy screeched. 'We'll get caught!'

Desperately looking over his shoulder, he spent the whole of the motorway journey terrified that the police were going to see us.

I eventually told him – the next day – that I had passed my test!

Slowly things started to go wrong between us, and to be honest, it was mainly my fault. Jimmy was very involved with the farm and I am sure that with the two very young children, I became preoccupied and tired. Eventually, I was unable to feel that I could stay with Jimmy for the rest of my life and so, taking my girls with me, I left.

In the early 1970s, to walk out on your husband was a different story from now. Some people would not have you in their house. It carried a lot of stigma and because of that I am most grateful for the support that my parents gave me, irrespective of their own thoughts. I am sure that I hurt Jimmy very much, and it is one part of my life that I truly regret for the unhappiness I caused. I just married too young and we grew apart. Jimmy is now remarried with a second family and, I believe, very happy.

So, here was I, with two small children, requiring a job. A large hotel in the town where I was living was advertising for a receptionist so, without further ado, I applied. Within days a letter arrived offering me an interview.

Dressed in a suit to impress, I arrived at the hotel and asked at reception for the manager. The plush carpets and fine furniture were a different world to me.

'The manager will be with you in a minute,' the receptionist told me, 'perhaps you would like to wait in the lounge.'

'Thank you,' I said, and wandered over to the seats by the large window overlooking the Bristol Channel.

'Mrs Nichols?' a voice called.

I turned and the young manager, in a smart grey suit, directed me through to his office.

I sat in the chair in front of his desk; he pulled his chair forward, sliding his pad to the middle of his desk ready to write down my details.

Mr Barry put me at ease. In his soft Irish voice he explained about the kind of hotel it was, the way that they worked and the kind of person they were looking for. Then he started to ask me questions to see what I could do.

'Have you used an accounting machine?' he asked.

'No,' I replied.

'Have you ever used a switchboard?' Mr Barry enquired.

'No,' I replied.

'Have you ever done wages – PAYE or Kalamazoo?' He tilted his head, raising his eyebrows.

'No,' I replied. I was beginning to feel uncomfortable.

'Have you ever done accounting or ledger work?' His pen, that had been poised to write down all my qualifications, was put down.

'How about typing, can you type?' He was really trying to find something I could do.

'I can, but very slow.' I could see this was going nowhere.

'Let's try again,' he said, smiling. 'What *can* you do?'

Laughing, I said: 'I can milk cows!'

Amazingly – I got the job.

2

From Housekeeping to Husbandry

Once you decide to take a career in the hotel and catering trade, anything and everything becomes possible. Although, over a period of time, you learn how to do the job you were employed for, there will always be the odd crisis that will find you helping either in the restaurant, behind the bar or in the kitchen, and even making beds.

One of the most important skills is to look as if everything is under control, when underneath you know that this is far from the truth. (I am sure that anyone who has worked in a hotel will know that John Cleese's wonderful programme, 'Fawlty Towers', is not so far from reality as you would imagine.) The art of confidence I was to learn from Miss Sheena Brown.

I had only been at the hotel for a matter of a few months when I was told by Mr Barry that a new head receptionist was due to start. Frank, our head waiter, well known for his practical jokes, sauntered up from the restaurant and leant on the reception counter.

'I hear you've got a new head receptionist starting next week,' he casually remarked.

'Yes,' I said, 'I've just been told.'

'You don't know her name by any chance, do you?' he asked.

'I think Mr Barry said it was a Sheena Brown,' I replied.

'Oh no,' he gasped, 'not Sheena Brown from er, from er . . .' Frowning, he scratched his head as if trying to remember.

'I think it was Bristol, why?' I asked, concerned that this name provoked such a response.

'Oh, my God, it *is* the same person!' he said in mock horror. He was winding me up, good and proper, and I fell for it. By the time Miss Sheena Brown was due to arrive, I was on hot coals.

Unbeknown to me, the day before coming, all of Sheena's friends from the hotel she was leaving had given her a farewell party. The day that she arrived, Sheena was suffering quite acutely with a hangover. Miss Brown was short and casually dressed; she had blonde hair and what appeared a very severe face.

I greeted her as she arrived. 'Good afternoon, can I help you?'

Trying her level best to stop her head from swimming around, Sheena said: 'Sheena Brown, you are expecting me. Have you got my keys?'

I felt I had never met such a sour-faced person in all my life, although a lot of it was the fear that Frank had so beautifully worked up. Not a smile, not a glimmer of friendliness – I was quite sure that I was never going to get on with her!

'I'll just call the porter to help you with your bags,' I trilled, moving over to the intercom to call the porter. I tripped over the chair with nervousness and, to make matters worse, the porter did not answer my call. I was sure that the poker-faced Sheena had already decided how inefficient I was. With the blood rising in my face, I made the excuse of going to find the porter and ran down the corridor looking for him. He had just come up from the cellar, so motioning frantically to him to come quickly, I was able to send Sheena away with the porter to her room.

I was so upset. Over the short period that I had been there I had loved my work in the hotel, but I was quite sure now that there was no future there for me working with Miss Sheena Brown.

Within two weeks, the whole matter was resolved. I had found out that all of Frank's remarks had been a practical joke, and that it had only been through Sheena's self-inflicted illness that she had appeared so stern and arrogant. I was to embark on a friendship that continued from the other side of the world and back again and that remains as strong now as ever – despite our completely different interests and background.

We have the same sense of humour but I do not quite share the nerves of steel. Anyone who has Sheena as a true friend will be told quite categorically if they do something wrong, but will also be protected and cared for in a way that normally only a mother could.

If Frank thought he was good at practical jokes, Sheena was way ahead, in a different league. She once carried out a practical joke on our other receptionist, Jean, at a time when there had been a lot of publicity about immigrants coming into the country without proper permits.

It was Sheena's day off and she rang through to the hotel, speaking to Jean in a false voice, enquiring as to the prices of our bedrooms. Sheena explained that she and her 'clients' would be arriving late as the boat was not coming in until after dark, somewhere around 10.30 p.m. Jean quoted the prices, to which Sheena said they seemed quite high but her clients probably wouldn't mind sleeping ten to a bedroom, which would make it a lot cheaper. Jean said she was not sure if they could do that, and began to hesitate over taking the booking – perhaps she ought to check with the manager first. That was fine, said Sheena, because the boats were very slow, so they wouldn't be coming in for a few days – she would ring back.

You can imagine the mirth in the office on Sheena's return, when all this was repeated not only to her but to a very worried manager as well, who was on the verge of drawing up contingency plans until Sheena explained that it had been her on the telephone making the booking.

We were able to pay Sheena back when an elderly lady arrived at the hotel for her week's holiday. Our hotel was popular with elderly visitors, and we were used to unusual requests at times, such as being able to supply a commode to the room. (There was only one chambermaid, Mrs Hucker, who was prepared to deal with these pans in the mornings, and she was well known for her champagne parties!)

When this particular lady arrived Sheena was on duty at the desk. Signing herself in, the lady asked if anyone would be able to assist her when she undressed at night. Sheena delicately explained that although we tried to offer as much help as possible, this was not a request that had ever arisen before. Lowering her voice, the

19

lady explained that it was not actually to undress her, but she unfortunately had a false leg and required assistance just to take it off. With her mothering instincts coming out, Sheena confided that she would help.

'Typical,' said Sheena, after the lady had gone up to her room. 'It always has to be me on duty when these things happen!'

True to her word, later that evening, Sheena went and helped the lady remove the false limb, which was leant against the wall in the lobby of her suite. When she returned to the office Sheena went into graphic detail of what she had had to do. 'And,' she said in a pained voice, 'I've even got to go and put it back on in the morning!'

Waiting until it was quite late and the lady was sure to be asleep, Jean and I borrowed a pass-key and went quietly up to the lady's bedroom. Carefully opening the door, we could see that there, just inside, as described by Sheena, was the artificial leg leaning against the wall. Quickly and quietly, we stole the false leg.

In the morning, Jean and I were busy sorting out the bills ready for our guests who were leaving that day. Sheena had already gone up to the room to help the lady dress. Ashen-faced, she returned to reception. 'Everything all right?' I casually remarked.

'You're not going to believe this,' said Sheena, with her hand holding her forehead. 'It's gone.'

'What's gone?' said Jean, glancing at me.

'Her leg,' said Sheena, incredulously, 'her flipping leg. I can't believe it! I know, I leant it against the wall. How can anyone lose a false leg?'

'Sounds very careless to me,' I quipped. Jean looked away, knowing that she wouldn't be able to keep a straight face if our eyes had met. 'What have you told her?' I asked.

'I just made the excuse that I had remembered something important, but I'm going to have to go back soon,' wailed Sheena.

'Have you asked the porter?' I questioned. 'Maybe he collected it with the shoes for cleaning.'

'Don't be silly,' Sheena snapped.

'Oh, wait a minute, I'm sure I saw a leg over here just now,' said Jean, rummaging through the boxes in the corner and producing the limb in question.

'You ********s!' said Sheena, as Jean and I collapsed laughing together.

'Yes,' said Jean, 'but you should have seen your face!'

While I was working, my mother helped me look after my two girls who were still very young, only 2 and 3 years old. Then my mother became ill and I began to realize how much I had depended on her. I had the alternative of paying someone to look after them, but financial help was very hard to come by in those days. It was becoming apparent that I was going to find it very difficult to cope with the upbringing of my two girls on my own.

The courts had awarded custody to be equally shared between Jimmy and myself: I had them Monday to Friday and Jimmy was having them for the weekends, but the girls were finding this very unsettling, especially Kerry, the younger.

I decided, after much heartache, to give them up. At their age, I knew they would have very little memory of me and it would be better for them to have a stable background. Other than sending birthday and Christmas presents, I intended to have no contact. Jimmy was very happy to have them back. I loved them both dearly, which is why I was prepared to let them go.

Both of my girls renewed contact with me as they became young women although, as my parents stayed in touch with them throughout, I was always aware of how they were. I am lucky that we now have a close relationship despite the fact that I missed seeing them grow up. Jimmy brought them up well. I am proud to have one daughter, Kerry, in the mounted police force and another daughter, Wendy, who is multilingual, living in Germany and working for British Airways.

Around the same time, Sheena received the visa that she had been waiting for, and she was soon to be on her way to Australia. It was time to move on, away from painful memories, and I managed to get a job at a hotel in the Lake District.

I had never seen such beautiful countryside. Tall rugged mountains stood high in the distance as large expanses of woodland covered the sides of the hills. Every turn of the twisting roads seems to bring a different view, from waterfalls rushing down the side of moss-laden stone boulders to the shimmering calm waters of the lakes. It was a totally different lifestyle, much slower, so restful, so quiet.

The hotel I came to was a very old one, and it was the first time that I had actually 'lived in' (which means that my accommodation was included in my wages). My room was like a little bed-sit. I was shown where the stillroom was, so that if I wanted to, I could go and make a coffee.

I unpacked my belongings and, before I knew it, it was already quite late in the evening. I decided to make my way down to the stillroom; everywhere was quiet and I did not meet anyone as I walked through the corridors.

Arriving at the stillroom, I pushed open the door and found that the light was out. Fumbling up the side of the wall looking for a light switch, I found nothing. Peering in the dark, I could just see the still simmering over on the other side of the room. It is a large stainless steel container where the water is constantly kept on the boil ready for serving teas and coffees. The gas jet, heating the water, was throwing out just enough light for me to see the silhouette of the cups and saucers, so I thought I could manage without a light.

Walking across the floor, I could feel something gritty under my feet. Somebody, I thought, has spilt some sugar and hasn't cleared it up. I had just made it to the still when the night porter barged into the room, immediately switching the light on in a practised manner as he obviously knew where it was.

He gave out an involuntary scream, surprised to see me standing there. But he was not the only one: I also gave out an involuntary scream, as when the light flooded the stillroom I could plainly see the 'spilt sugar' scuttling under any available cover. It had been cockroaches!

We both put our fingers to our lips to stop the other from screaming at the same time. Laughing, we then introduced ourselves to each other. It was evidently the main source of amusement at night for the night porters to sit on the fridges in the stillroom and switch the lights out, and then after a while turn the lights back on and see how many cockroaches they could flatten before they disappeared!

Well, I thought, my first contact with wildlife in the Lake District. There are six species of cockroaches, three of which are native to Britain; these are more commonly found in woods in southern England and are hardly ever seen. The three species which have arrived from abroad prefer warmer conditions, and these are the ones to be found in kitchens and bakeries. These days, though, with modern pesticides and higher hygiene standards, they can be kept under control. The main difficulty with them is that they can flatten their bodies so well that they can fit in very small cracks and crevices. What's more, as they are nocturnal, only coming out at night to feed on food scraps left lying around, it is not until there are quite a few of the little souls that you realize you have a problem. A cockroach walking about in a dining-room is not good news – neither is a mouse.

We had one incident where a young lady was sitting on her own in the dining-room eating her lunch, when one of the waitresses noticed to her horror that a little mouse was sitting under the table, also enjoying his lunch. It was decided that the best course of action was to do nothing. Luckily the mouse finished his lunch first and, in the absence of a napkin to wipe his mouth with, ran off with biscuit crumbs still on his whiskers, back to his hiding place under a chest of drawers. He was evacuated later in the day, when the restaurant was closed.

On my days off, I explored as much of the countryside as I could. The further away I could get from the main towns, the more attractive unspoilt areas could be found. I never managed to find the deer while I was up there, but I did see red squirrels. There are so few of these now as they are almost totally dependent on mature woodland consisting of conifers. It is the conifer, particularly the Scots pine, that supplies them with nearly all their food as they eat the cones, the young shoots, and also the bark of these trees. Red squirrels are found in some deciduous woodland but then they need hazel for the nuts and some conifers for the seeds in their cones.

Grey squirrels have been blamed for the reduction in numbers of red squirrels, but the truth of the matter is just that they are a hardier animal and not so shy, which means that there are many more suitable habitats for them.

The red squirrel has the lovely tufts to its ears, which are more noticeable in the winter, and a striking white tummy and red bushy tail. Living nearly all their lives up in the trees, and being very shy, they are difficult to see; but it is said that in the mating season the male makes a sneezing sound which attracts other males to the area and they all go off in a gang looking for a female. So be warned – if you have a heavy cold, and go out walking in the Lake District, you could have a good chance of being joined by some red squirrels. (I expect chasing the female is optional!)

It was on one of my days off, travelling near Lake Bassenthwaite, that I saw my first kingfisher. He was sitting on a branch, watching the flow of water running underneath him. I had never seen anything so colourful. Quietly leaning over the branch, I watched, fascinated. The bill of this bird seems almost as long as the bird is tall, and the iridescent blue of his head and wings contrast with the orange body.

Suddenly he swooped further up the stream as if he was following something in the water, and almost too quickly for me to keep track of him he dived into the water and emerged with a small but worthwhile trophy. Then he was gone.

Very often kingfishers will make a hole in the wet banks of a stream; literally by flying at the bank with their beaks and gouging out the mud, they slowly create a tunnel. The tunnel can be anything from 6 inches to 40 inches long before they create the chamber for the eggs to be laid. Two and sometimes even three broods may be reared in a season.

The kingfisher tends always to fish in the same sites and this is how some of the incredible filming of the little bird diving to catch his prey has been achieved. One photographer filled a glass tank with fish and placed it in a stream where a kingfisher was known to hunt; slowly, over a period of six months, the tank was very gradually raised. The fish stock was replenished in the tank most days, and no doubt the kingfisher welcomed having the constant food supply so readily available. The tank was eventually raised high enough for the cameraman to be able to film not only the entry of the kingfisher into the water, but the complete dive and the kingfisher emerging with the fish. Clever stuff!

Transport by bus in the Lake District is not very easy and as our hotel was away from the main town, you would often be asked by other members of staff to get something for them, if they knew you were going to town. Once, I was off to Kendal to do some shopping. Nigel, our chef, was tackling his car that day; there was something wrong with the exhaust and he was endeavouring to mend it.

I needed to change buses at Keswick, one of the smaller towns. The journey there and back was going to take most of the day, but I always enjoyed the trip as it was all breathtaking scenery. We passed many small farm cottages and hillsides that were divided up by dry stone walls as far as the eye could see. At some points the grass gave way to rough terrain where the bracken covered most of the land which reached up to the craggy tops of the mountains. There was no need to divide the land in the scrubby areas as so little could be grazed there. Sheep were dotted around and I always wondered how the farmer knew where to find them. When I got talking to a local, he explained that the sheep belong to the farm, being the same stock that have been bred from for many generations. They will not wander very far from the farm where they were reared. The sheep will remain together as a flock, and in turn will teach their lambs, as they run at foot, the territory that belongs to them. This is so unlike sheep in other parts of the country that can be sold from one farm to another, as they are put into fields and can be contained. Here the sheep always remain on the same farm; indeed, if you wanted to sell your farm, then you would have to leave your sheep behind too, otherwise there would be a lot of confused sheep walking about.

Having done all my shopping, I was on my return journey. When I arrived at the bus station at Keswick to wait for the connection, I noticed a blackboard by the office with my name on it, saying there was a message for me in the office. On enquiring, I was asked to ring Nigel back at the hotel. Wondering what was wrong, I telephoned only to be told that he had found the repair slightly more complicated than he had imagined; was it possible for me to get a part at Keswick Motors? It was impossible for him to get into Keswick, collect the part and get home in time to fit it. So, taking the part number, I agreed to collect it.

When I got to the garage, I realized that I had not got very much money on me. The garage was very busy, and a middle-aged man came to the counter and asked if he could help. Explaining the situation, I told him the make of the car and gave him the part number – I also hesitantly asked him the price. When he told me it was nearly £30, I was crestfallen – I did not have that much on me, nor was I carrying my cheque book.

'That's all right,' the garage man said helpfully, 'I know where you live, I'll trust you.'

'Well, that's ever so kind of you,' I replied gratefully and he went to fetch the part for me.

When he returned, I began to wish he had not been so trusting. It was the exhaust and pipe complete, which was just over eight feet long. Sliding it over the counter, he told me to 'Mind how you go.'

And I was left holding this enormous part. Let me tell you that walking through town with an eight-foot exhaust does tend to make people notice you. I felt even more of a fool when I arrived at the bus station, and one of the drivers came over and suggested that I went into the office to see if I would be allowed on to the bus with such a large object.

For ten minutes the staff pored over an official manual before deciding that it would be classed as a dangerous obstacle and I could therefore not take it on the bus. They suggested I called a taxi. Trying to look as if I had the whole situation under control, I walked out of the office – a member of staff holding the door open for me so that I could get my 'luggage' out without injuring anyone – and made my way to the telephone box. Leaning the exhaust against the booth, I went inside and called for a taxi.

A gentleman answered the phone.

'Can I have a taxi to just outside Bassenthwaite?' I asked.

'Certainly Madam, where from?' came the reply.

'I'm at the bus station in Keswick,' I explained.

'Are you ready for the taxi now?' he politely asked.

'Yes, please,' I replied.

'How will I recognize you?' came the question.

'Quite easy,' I said with gritted teeth, 'I shall be standing by the telephone box with an eight-foot exhaust part in my hand!'

Sometimes favours can go just too far.

I had wondered, when I arrived at the Lake District in the autumn, why some of the roads were so wide. With the arrival of summer and the incredible influx of visitors, it became all too apparent. I had seen the lovely rich autumn reds and browns change to the snow-capped bleak winter scenes, followed by the burst of spring flowers and new green leaves. Now it had become coaches, cream teas, and icecream. It was time for a change again: I was off to Sussex.

From assistant manageress of a hotel to manageress of a pub/restaurant was a different lifestyle again. I was working for a man who had several public houses that he had turned into eating houses, which in the 1970s was quite a new thing. I moved around several of the establishments over a period of time and enjoyed them all.

One of the pub/restaurants in the group was the Hole in the Wall at Seaford, which was a seaside town. We were dealing with the holiday trade. Some of the staff were Spanish, and one young waiter in particular was very loyal to me and followed me to most of the places I moved to. Pepe spoke very little English but he tried hard, and we endeavoured to teach him different words as we went along. He was short with dark curly hair, very polite and good at his job. I realized how little English he could read when he presented me with a lovely Christmas card from him and his girlfriend, with 'Happy Christmas to my Darling Wife' written across the front.

Tony and Espe were a Spanish couple who helped in the kitchen, and Ern was our kitchen porter – he would do all the washing up and keep the kitchen clean. Ern often went fishing from the sea wall at high tide and would bring his catches back. I hated to see the fish flipping around in a bowl gasping and usually kept out of the way until they had sorted it out.

On this particular evening, Espe had felt sorry for a fish that Ern had brought home and was sitting in a chair up to the table in the kitchen with a large bowl of water. Using two forks, she was cradling the fish in the water trying to revive it. As soon as she took the forks away it went on its side, and so with dedication she cradled it again, keeping it upright.

'Shame, isn't it?' I said to Espe, screwing up my face with distaste. 'I don't know why he doesn't bang them on the head.'

27

'He look better now,' Espe said in her broken English, watching the fish in the bowl. I left her to it.

Going through the kitchen half an hour later, there was a distinct aroma of cooked fish in the air. Espe was still sitting at the table but the bowl was gone; so too were the forks, which were now replaced by a knife and fork. The fish which I vaguely recognized was now cooked and partly eaten.

'Espe!' I said, quite shocked.

'Oh! He no live, I eat,' she said, tucking into her supper. So much for sentiment.

The Barley Mow was one of the places I liked the most, perhaps because the restaurant was done out as a cowstall (!) – the tables were placed in stalls with the cows' brass name plates on the sides. It was quite a high-class restaurant in those days, and in the evenings at weekends I was expected to wear long evening dress while taking orders and showing people through to their tables.

We had a very young commis chef, who was rather difficult to train – you had to struggle to find jobs that he was capable of doing. It was a Saturday night so we were going to be busy, and as usual he appeared, with the little words 'is there anything I can do?' tripping off his lips. With Chef's remarks from only a few minutes before – 'keep him away from me or I'll kill him' – still ringing in my ears, I suggested that maybe he could sort out the sweet trolley.

'It's nearly all done, the gateaux are on there, check that the jugs of cream are full, that the serving spoons are ready, then garnish a plate (meaning put a doily on it) and put out the cream eclairs. Then you can put it through into the dining-room. Can you do that?' I asked.

Smiling, he nodded, pleased that he had been trusted to do something.

Nearly half an hour later, Chef told me that the first meal was ready and I ushered the party through into the dining-room towards their table. There in its usual place stood the sweet trolley and sitting proudly on their garnished plate – on a bed of lettuce, with sliced tomatoes and cucumber sprinkled around them – were the chocolate eclairs.

I was totally in agreement with Chef!

My job obviously depended on making a success of the business and making profits on the food and drink. I was therefore very interested when a young salesman came in offering me a half a pig at a very reasonable price. It came complete but I was sure that Chef would be able to butcher it, and so I snapped up the bargain. The young man very kindly carried this side of pork in for me and hung it in the meat fridge. Chef was on his day off, but I would tell him the next day. I paid the man from petty cash, and he was soon gone.

Bridget, the cleaner, had been in the bar when he arrived and saw the half-pig going through to the meat larder.

'Sure, 'twas a lovely piece of meat for that price,' she trilled in her Irish lilt.

'Yes,' I replied, 'it was very reasonable.' This was sure to help the profits.

It couldn't have been more than an hour later that Mr Martin, who owned the chain of pubs, rang on his weekly check-up to see if all was well. He was one of those people who, when he came to visit, would point out straightaway if a light bulb had blown or something was not in its right place.

The bookings were coming in nicely, no problems with the staff: he had the art of asking all the right questions to make sure all was well.

'Jolly good, then, Pauline,' he said, 'I'm pleased with the way things are going. By the way, we've heard that someone is going round with some stolen meat, so if anyone comes in offering you any, don't take it.'

'Right,' I said, with an uncomfortable vision of the half-pig hanging in the meat larder. 'Bye then.' I replaced the telephone.

I could not believe this was happening to me. What the hell was I going to do? Just then Bridget came through having finished her daily chores.

'Right,' she said, 'I'm all done, 'twill be tomorrow before I see ye again.'

'I don't suppose, Bridget,' I said hesitantly, 'that you'd be interested in that side of pork?'

'Are ye not wanting it then?' she asked.

'Well,' – I shrugged my shoulders – 'I hadn't realized that Chef had ordered one as well and . . .'

''T would be lovely,' she said, 'specially for that price, but I could'ne take it unless it's been cut up.'

'No problem,' I said, thinking it couldn't be that difficult. 'I'll have it ready by about 4 p.m. if you want to pick it up.'

'You're a lovely gel,' she beamed. 'I'll be in around 4.'

I could not wait to get rid of all the customers after lunch. The thought of the side of pork in the larder made me feel guilty every time it crept into my mind.

As soon as everyone had gone, I rushed upstairs and got my cookery book. I was sure there was a picture in the front showing the joints. Yes! I was right. Running down the stairs, I laid the book on the table and went to get the offending half-pig.

Half a pig, let me tell you, is quite a big and heavy object and the young man had hung it on two stainless steel meat hooks, each one going the other way on the metal rod. Trying to lift the weight with my shoulders, no sooner did I get one hook off than the other would go back on. I battled with this blasted pig for nearly ten minutes before freeing it from the rail. The complete thing folded over me, and I staggered into the kitchen and hoisted it on to the table. Placing it up the same way as the book, I studied the cuts.

Covering its face with a teacloth, so it couldn't watch me, I set about reducing it to joints. A couple of the pieces looked unsightly, but by the time I had tied them up as joints they looked quite presentable. It was when I got to the huge leg joint that I was thrown. I wasn't too sure where or how to attack it, so deciding that to do nothing was the best policy, I left it. I bagged it all up and was only just finishing when Bridget arrived.

Now with all the names fresh in my mind, I went through all the joints with her until we got to this large leg joint.

'Now,' I said, patting the joint in the bag, 'I wasn't sure just how big your family was, or whether, as it was such a nice piece of meat, you would save it until you had a large gathering, so I thought it best to leave this joint whole.'

'Sure, that's lovely,' said Bridget, 'I don't know how to tank ye enough.'

'Don't mention it,' I murmured as I helped her carry the meat out to the car.

Problem solved, I leant against the door as I came back into the kitchen. In my hand was the cash to replace the petty cash. With luck, now that the meat was in smaller pieces, no one would recognize it as the half a pig that arrived in the morning. I never did find out if in fact it was part of the stolen consignment. But then, I never really told anyone about it – until now . . .

Among the more unusual regulars who frequented the bar was a witches' coven that lived locally. I always got on very well with them and found them interesting to talk to. It was white magic that they practised and they did at times do animal healing. When I left, they presented me with a yellow glass disc, depicting the sun, which I still have. The glass face is about twelve inches across, so it is quite large. It was, they said, to bring me luck and happiness.

In all this time Sheena had kept in touch with me and, through her letters, I had heard about her travels as she explored Australia. It was nearing the time for her two years over there to come to an end, and just at that time I had the chance of taking over an old pub within the group, one that desperately needed modernizing. I would need a partner so I contacted Sheena, and she agreed to join me on her return to England.

The Berwick Inn had been closed for over ten years, and when we moved in it was like stepping back in time. The man who had owned it had lost interest in it many years before and when the place was closed, the key in the door was turned and all the pumps, bottles and furniture were just left.

We had a super time, turning out all the rooms and discovering all kinds of relics – including the outside toilet which, as we found once we had cleared away all the undergrowth, was a bench with a pot in it. The pan was in willow pattern!

Although we had been friends for some time, it was the first time we had actually lived together and it took time to get used to each other's ways. I fall out of bed in the same mood as I fell in, but Sheena finds the mornings very difficult and to hold a conversation before 10 a.m. was practically impossible. My constant singing nearly drove her up the wall!

Just before Sheena arrived back from Australia, I had purchased a red setter puppy and called her Sheena, which did in time lead to problems. As with all red setters, she took a long time to train; despite being six months old, there was still the occasional mishap at night. Why it should be Sheena who always seemed to find these puddles in the morning walking around with her socks on, I'll never know. The setter was also prone to pulling the washing off the washing line, and Sheena was convinced that most of her jumpers reached her knees instead of her waist because the dog had been hanging on them while they were drying.

The pub was right by a railway station and often a train would be stationary, right by our small garden at the side of the building. The garden was mainly lawn, with a circular fishpond in the middle. One day the auburn-haired nuisance had been nosing around in the bedroom upstairs and unbeknown to us had found a drawer open with a full box of tampons. Taking this prize out on to the lawn, she emptied the box and was gaily playing with all the tubes that had been inside.

Noticing her frolicking around, we both wondered what she was up to and went out to see. On seeing us coming out, the setter was sure we had come to join in, and prancing down on her front legs she wagged her tail. With a tampon in her mouth looking like a white cigar with a thin white string trailing from it, we realized what she had. We were also very conscious of the faces watching us from a stationary train waiting for the lights to change on the railway line. With the disadvantage of a fishpond to dance round we did two circuits trying to catch the wretched dog, and then decided on withdrawal until the train, plus spectators, had gone. It was so embarrassing!

I'm sure the one thing that Sheena will remember most about the setter was taking it out in the car. At that time I had a Mini Traveller, and the setter was used to travelling in the back with the seat down. She had also got into the habit of travelling standing up, and just resting her head on my shoulder.

When Sheena came, the dog would stand in the back as usual; but as Sheena was shorter in the body than me, when she was driving the dog would rest her head on top of Sheena's. This gave the appearance of Sheena wearing a Sherlock Holmes-type auburn hat with the dog's ears coming down either side of her head like

flaps. What annoyed Sheena even more was that when she got to a junction and had to look right and left, the dog managed to turn with her so that the dog did not have to move her head.

Not very far away from the pub was Arlington Reservoir where I would often walk the dog for exercise. The area was very open, and even on a summer's day there seemed to be a cool wind blowing. The reservoir was not used for any leisure activities and was therefore always a quiet spot to walk. The one thing I can remember more vividly than anything was the beautiful sound of the skylarks as they trilled their distinctive song spiralling up into the sky, sometimes so high they appeared just as brown specks although their song could be clearly heard. The skylark is quite a plain little bird with brown colouring. Unlike most birds, it sings on the wing and therefore is able to mark out its territory on the ground by circling and singing above it. In this way it is able to colonize large open ground areas which other birds, if they require a post to sing from to claim their territory, are unable to inhabit. Probably for this reason the skylark is the most widely spread bird species to be found in Britain and Ireland. They are ground-nesting birds, and I had to keep an eye on the setter, in case she came across a nest created just in a small dip in the ground. The nest is made out of dry coarse grass and roots, and is then lined with softer grass and sometimes even hair. I have seen the nests with the pretty speckled eggs; and once the setter came upon a nest with some tiny fledglings, but the parent bird dived and tried to divert her attention, so I was soon aware of what was going on and called her away.

The skylark is mainly vegetarian, feeding on tiny shoots, and does therefore cause some damage to crops, but I'm sure that in return for that beautiful bird-song, we can forgive them for the small amount of damage that they do. Sadly, this is now scarcely necessary, since these once-plentiful birds have become almost rare, and any sighting is welcomed.

We were lucky to have a choice of walks near to us, being able either to go to the reservoir or to walk through the Forestry Commission land. There is talk of the Forestry Commission becoming privatized, but it would be a great shame if these areas were no longer open to the public for them to walk in and enjoy.

Slowly the pub began to take shape as the alterations neared completion. The arrival of a deep fat fryer was Sheena's ultimate joy as she was convinced that you could cook just about everything in it. I had my doubts, even after she explained that you could fry an egg in it as long as you did not lift the basket up before the white had solidified.

After the episode of Sheena trying to make packet soup through the coffee machine (it didn't work!), I had my doubts about leaving her to do any of the cooking. Eventually the pub was opened and trade slowly began to build up. Lunchtimes in the middle of the week were usually quiet and it was difficult always to have a wide selection of food available. A couple passing by called in for lunch and ordered two scotch eggs with salad. Having taken their order, I left the bar serving area, going down the four stairs that led to the kitchen.

'Two scotch eggs and salad,' I called to Sheena who was sorting out a delivery that had just arrived.

'Oh, damn,' she said, 'I think they are all frozen.'

'I'll go and tell them we haven't got any,' I said.

'No,' said Sheena, keen not to upset anyone, 'I'll pop them in the fryer, they will soon defrost.'

'But they will be warm!' I replied.

'Just go and tell them that they are being cooked fresh and they are nearly ready but do they mind them being warm,' said Sheena – she had an answer for everything.

Going back up to the bar, I explained to the couple and no, that was fine, they were in no hurry anyway.

Putting my head round the door, I gave Sheena a thumbs-up sign down in the kitchen.

After five minutes, I went down to see how she was getting on. The scotch eggs looked decidedly crisp and as Sheena cut them in half to present them on the plate, half the scotch egg shot across the kitchen. It was still frozen in the middle.

'What are we going to do now?' asked Sheena.

'Don't worry,' I said, and going back to the bar, I went over to see the couple.

'I'm so sorry,' I apologized to the couple, 'but Chef has just taken the scotch eggs out and they really are not up to the standard that we like to keep to. I would really rather you chose something else. We will do it as quickly as possible.'

It was no trouble, they said, and they both then chose some toasted sandwiches.

Darting down to the kitchen again, I told Sheena what I had done, and she set about doing the sandwiches.

The couple by now had been waiting some time, so I went over to pass the time of day with them. We talked about the pub only just opening and I explained that Sheena was new in the kitchen and as yet was still finding where everything was. (She had in fact been there six months!)

'I'll just go and check, as I'm sure they must be ready now,' I said, moving away.

As I went down to the kitchen, Sheena was just putting the final touches to the food.

'It's OK,' I placated her, 'I've told them you're new.'

Back in the bar, I was polishing the glasses when the door from the kitchen opened as Sheena came up with the food. Carrying the tray in, Sheena stared around the room and uttered: 'Is this the bar?'

Thankfully the couple did enjoy their meal, and did come back again.

We spent a fun-filled year building up the trade, and although I was on many occasions called away to help at other establishments within the group, in the main we were together.

I was then to meet up with Mac, who came to work at the pub as a barman. He had just left the Royal Air Force and was hoping to start a career in the licensed trade. When the chance arose to go and run a holiday camp in Norfolk, we decided to make a go of it together. We moved to a small village called Hopton on Sea with a population that changed from two to three thousand in the winter to about 45,000 in the summer.

It took a while to get used to the vastness of the job. On our holiday camp alone there were over 200 chalets as well as another 150 caravans, all of which had to be ready for the Easter season. Even a simple task such as going around and flushing the toilets to make sure they all worked took one person two days to do.

Summer was a whirlwind of bar work, cabaret and children's parties, all totally exhausting. Much of what you do does tend to be repetitive and I can remember in 1975 and 1976, when we had two exceptionally hot summers, we had terrible trouble with ants going into the chalets. Behind the reception desk stood boxes and boxes of ant powder, ready to hand out to anyone who came and complained. The conversation always went like this.

'Good morning, sir, can I help you?'

'I hope so,' the camper would remark, 'we have a lot of ants in our chalet.'

'I'm so sorry,' came the pat reply, 'we have had such a dry

summer this year that it has become quite a problem, but here is some ant powder, which you can shake just where they are coming in.'

'Will it kill them?' was always the reply.

'Oh, yes, but please let us know if you have any further problems.' Say it with a smile, we were told, and they will go away happy.

Once you have repeated this thirty times in one day the devil creeps into you, and twice the temptation to change the patter was just too much.

'Good morning, sir, can I help you?' I greeted the camper.

'I hope so,' said the guest. 'We've got a lot of ants in our chalet.'

'I'm so sorry sir, but it has been such a dry summer this year that it is becoming quite a problem. Here is some ant powder that you can shake just where they are coming in.'

'Will it kill them?' asked the camper.

It was too much – 'No,' I replied, 'but it will slow them down and you can squash them more easily.'

'Oh!' said the camper, and off he went.

When the next one came in, I finally snapped.

'Good morning, sir, can I help you?' I greeted.

'We've got an awful lot of ants in our chalet,' came the reply.

'But, are they quiet?' I asked.

'Beg your pardon?' the camper said, taken aback.

'Are they quiet?' I repeated.

'Well, yes,' answered the man, quizzically.

'Thank goodness for that,' I sighed. 'It's when you get them marching in, with the one in front throwing the baton up in the air followed by the brass band behind, they can get very noisy.'

Luckily we shared the same sense of humour and he laughed. He still received his tub of ant powder, but there are only so many times that you can be asked the same question before it gets to you!

Mac and I married and lived just a short distance from the camp, up a lane in the last of a line of four terraced cottages. Ours was nearest to the sea and all I had to do was go out of the front door and down a grass track to arrive at the sandy cliffs overlooking the beach.

Autumn and winter still continued to be my favourite seasons as then I would have the beach all to myself and could walk along the golden sands with the North Sea crashing in large waves on the shore – and oh, those cold winds! There were times when it was almost impossible to walk along the beach without a scarf around your face, protecting it from the bitter cold.

From the beach, the cliffs hid the thousands of holiday homes stretching as far as the eye could see on the flat land. But even then the view would often be spoilt by the huge oil platforms that were often anchored just offshore.

It was during one of our morning walks that the red setter came upon something lying up against the wooden breakwater. She was some way ahead of me, but I could tell from the pricked-up ears and wagging tail that it was something to get excited about. Going down on her front legs, she was barking as though trying to get something to play. Hurrying up to her, I called her away.

It was the first one I had ever seen. A beautiful young baby grey seal. It was covered in a thick luxurious cream fur. The huge black eyes blinked, causing a watery film to slide over the eyes, almost giving the impression that it was going to cry. Moving away from it, I was both concerned that it was there on its own but at the same time entranced by this fat, cuddly-looking young pup. I am sure it only *looked* cuddly as grey seals can be very aggressive, particularly with young around, so I was careful in case the mother was still nearby.

Grey seal pups are born with this lovely cream coat but it only lasts for two to three weeks, until the pup is weaned, and then the distinct dapple colour of the adult comes through. A seal pup weighs around 15 kilograms when born (33 pounds) and in the short time it suckles from its mother, only two to three weeks, it will nearly treble its body weight. The milk from a seal is very rich, containing 50 per cent fat, compared with cow's milk which only contains 4 per cent, so it is hardly surprising that they are able to grow so quickly.

Walking back to the cottage, we left the seal pup alone. It appeared healthy enough and there was every chance that the mother would return, but I would check again in the afternoon to see if he was still there.

Grey seals are fascinating mammals, being able to stay under water for as long as thirty minutes without breathing. They are able to reduce their heartbeat from seventy or eighty beats per minute down to between five and ten. With special facilities to trap oxygen in the body they are able to contain most of the blood around the heart while still being able to use their brain and muscles to remain active.

They are long-living, too, with a female recorded as being as old as 46 years, although they rarely live over 35 years. The males are not so hardy! The record for a male is 26, but the usual age would be around 20 years old. Because so much of their life is spent in the sea it makes it very difficult to be able to record numbers, but it is estimated that the British population is approximately 75,000.

Our little pup was still there in the afternoon, so I rang the RSPCA to find out what we should do. They asked me to leave it until the next day but if it was still there then, I was to contact them. They were slightly concerned because it was not a known breeding place. Going down on my own the next morning I took a blanket, and as the seal pup was still in the same place on his own, I picked him up in the blanket and carried him home. He was collected within the hour and I hope he survived to be put back with his own kind.

My glass disc that I was given by the witches wasn't working and my second marriage was going dreadfully wrong, despite the birth of my son Simon. Four years after my second marriage, I found myself packing my bags again and leaving everything behind, except my son. Come hell or high water, I was not going to lose him. I could not go through again what I had suffered when I lost my girls. (Mind you, now that he is a strapping six-footer at university, phoning only when he needs money, I could change my mind!) I don't think this time it was my fault, but then there are always two sides to everything.

I returned yet again to my long-suffering parents, but determined to find somewhere to live as soon as possible. An advertisement in a local paper for a housekeeper required by a farmer with three small children soon found me the very happy home where Simon and I still live.

So I was back in Somerset, living on a small dairy farm that eventually changed to an open farm for visitors and became well known for wildlife care as I slowly grew more involved with that side of animal husbandry.

You would think that I would have had enough of marriage not to go in for it a third time, but when you find a husband as special as the one I have now, you reel him in fast! Derek has now put up with me for nearly twenty years, with his three children, Barry, Kelly and Daniel, and my son, Simon, growing up as one family.

We have actually managed to get rid of all of them now, with Kelly married, Barry living more abroad than at home helping underprivileged children, and Daniel and Simon at university. The farm has become a centre for people to come and see not only farm animals but wildlife creatures as well. Many orphaned and injured wild animals are brought in to us and our aim is always to return them to the wild. Much of our work is therefore done behind the scenes, as wildlife must be given peace and quiet to cope with the trauma of captivity whilst in care.

We have adapted the traditional buildings of this sixteenth-century farm for displays and interpretation as well as housing a varied assortment of animals from bats to dormice, from foxes to longhorn cattle. We want our visitors to feel that they are coming to spend time in the country at our home, where they will enjoy a day on a farm and find out how wildlife and farming can co-exist to create the countryside that we so love. In order to give the right atmosphere we have given up our home – well, the bottom floor of the farmhouse, which is used as a tearoom, having left all our antique furniture downstairs to complement the open fires and shining brass. We, poor souls, have had to squeeze into the eight bedrooms upstairs, changing the rooms into a kitchen, lounge, office, staff room and bedrooms – but we manage! (The orange boxes are hard to live with, though!)

Part of the cowshed has been made into an observation sett for badgers after I hand-reared some cubs in 1989 and released them on the farm. The idea was to give them the chance of freedom, but also there was the hope that they would stay. It was through the badgers that we made contact with Simon King, the well-known wildlife film-maker, who came here to film the badgers and has since had film locations at the farm.

One of our badgers, Bluebell, did stay and even had cubs in the observation sett, so we were able to watch them grow. She also took on other orphan cubs and looked after them. When the pressure of wildlife work became too expensive for us to manage we started a support group which we called the 'Bluebell Sett Wildlife Appeal' after Bluebell, because we felt that she was doing some of the care work herself. Simon King very kindly became the patron.

It has been hard work, and the venture of changing from farming to being a wildlife rescue centre has meant a tremendous input of capital with very little return. Financially, life has at times been made very difficult.

39

Still, I would not change my life now. I'm in my element, having the chance to have such contact with wild creatures. It may be hard work; there are good times and there are sad times, but there aren't many places where you can find a barn owl sitting in the kitchen, or a badger walking about the house, and even a red deer that keeps pinching bubble gum from the shop – but then this is Secret World.

3

Cricket

If there is one thing that Derek and I don't have in common, it has got to be our hobbies. In my spare time I love to be involved with the Badger Group but Derek's main interest is cricket. Since he was a young boy he has always had the dream of being a professional player, and day upon day was spent practising with a bat and ball. His cousin Brian would often come to stay and, as he shared this interest, fine sunny days were spent playing cricket and wet days indoors playing a cricket board game. I think, in a way, Derek has been disappointed that none of his sons have followed in this sport but certainly Brian's three young sons, Timothy, Neil and Nicholas, are very good players and you never know – we may see a Kidner in the Somerset team yet.

Derek is quite good at cricket, although the career never materialized. He played for the village team in his teens but, sadly, farming and cricket were not compatible, as just when the team needs you in the middle of summer, there is a field of hay waiting to be baled, and business must come before pleasure.

By the time the farm had progressed to silage-making in the 1980s, Derek was about 35 years old. Silage-making is done earlier in the year than hay and is a much faster process so this gave Derek more time in the middle of summer to think about playing cricket. He longed to join the East Huntspill cricket team again before he was too old. We did discuss the situation as it meant that he would be missing for most Saturday afternoons, thus leaving the milking to me, but that was no real problem; so the dreaded whites were purchased, complete with bat, gloves, leg pads and the 'protector' – East Huntspill had another dedicated team-mate.

Of course, as he had not played for some time, Derek did not exactly shine at the start. However, a freak accident, when a ball was bowled hitting him straight in the mouth causing £200 of dental work, seemed to sharpen his concentration and he went on to win the trophy for Batsman of the Year – an award he was very pleased to obtain, as you can imagine. When the accident happened, Derek was obviously quite shaken and all the lads came to check that he was all right. He began to feel quite faint and collapsed, swallowing his tongue in the process, causing him to choke. He said he could vaguely remember everyone standing around confused and not really knowing what to do. Paul Gass, one of the team, taking the initiative, quickly put his hand in Derek's mouth and pulled his tongue forward. Derek could remember hearing someone in the background offering the advice that 'you're not meant to do that', meaning that placing one's hand into a person's mouth when they are convulsing can run the risk of your being bitten. To this day, however, Derek has been very grateful for Paul's quick thinking, for he would not otherwise be here now. A good game cricket may be but it can also be very dangerous, and one can fully understand the reason behind the protective wear that we see the professionals armed with when they play.

I must confess. I find cricket a most boring sport and one of the conditions of Derek playing was that I would never have to watch! This results in a certain amount of chiding that carries on between us, each not fully understanding the interest of the other.

A few years ago, we were on holiday in Cornwall and as we were driving along, we saw several white objects dotted about in a green field. 'Oh, look,' said Derek, 'I think that's a cricket match in progress.'

'Well, if it is, pull in and you can watch – I'll have a sleep.' I

answered, having the ability to close my eyes and sleep anywhere. Much to my amusement, as we drew nearer we discovered that it was not a cricket match at all but some free-range white turkeys. As far as I was concerned that said it all!

About a year ago, in early spring, a friend of mine, Michael Woods, who is a badger consultant, asked if I would assist with some bait-marking one Sunday morning in Dorset. Keen to be involved, I agreed. Michael had been called in by developers to do a badger survey over an area where a new road was to be constructed. Badgers and their setts are now protected by law and provision must be made if it is necessary to move or close down any of the setts. This is all done under licence with either English Nature or MAFF (Ministry of Agriculture, Fisheries and Food).

When new roads are built, if they cut across a badger territorial path, the badger will continue to use that path even though this means crossing the road. This often results in the animal being run over or at the very least causing a vehicle to swerve, which could result in an accident. So if, during the construction of a road, something like a tunnel can be created as an underpass, and the badger can then be encouraged to use this and go under the road instead, this can save the lives of a whole social group of badgers which otherwise could easily be killed by traffic. If put in at construction stage there is little cost to this procedure and it obviously saves badger lives, if not those of humans as well.

There are two things that are important. One is that the under-pass is placed exactly where the badger paths run; obviously, when a road runs through a large area, it will go through the territories of more than one social group, so a tunnel must be placed in each area of each individual social group. How do we know which territorial area belongs to each badger social group? Well, believe it or not it is quite easy! Badgers mark out their territories with dung pits all around the perimeter. Where two territories meet, the adjoining badger groups will place dung pits alongside their neighbours', daring them to enter into their territory – if they do, they will fight and sometimes even kill each other. When carrying out a survey, Michael would initially walk the area to find all the badger setts in the location, marking them down on a map. He would also mark down if they were main setts, annexe setts, outliers or subsidiary setts. A badger uses alternative setts at different times of the year – an outlier situated near a field of maize would be used more when the crop is ready for harvesting (and eating!) and there's no point in walking further than one has to for a food supply. There would, however, be only one main sett in each territory which is the home that is most used and usually has the most entrances.

Once Michael had determined where all the main setts were, he would put food down over a period of time in front of each main sett. In the food, which usually consists of peanuts and syrup, are mixed small coloured pellets, using a different colour for each main sett. The idea is that the badgers come up from the sett and eat the food, colour pellets and all – mind you, on occasions there are little trails of coloured pellets, where the consuming badger spits out the inedible pieces as he walks away, but in general most of them are taken down.

Nature being what it is, over a period of two or three days, dung is then deposited in the dung pits positioned on the perimeters of their territories. It is then up to the 'die-hard' volunteers to go searching for these dung pits with the inevitable stick to wriggle around and find what colour pellets are in the poo! Michael uses a paper scraper so that he can spread and sieve through it all (really dedicated); other volunteers had knives, and one even had a knife from the cutlery drawer (I made a mental note of who this was, remembering never to go to their home for tea!)

As this Sunday in question loomed nearer I went down with a

heavy cold, but I did not want to let Michael down as it is easier to work in pairs. Dosed with cold remedies and frantically sucking throat sweets, I was adamant on the Saturday night that I would still go. Derek sat in the chair in the kitchen watching cricket on TV as I prepared my packed lunch for the next day. Intermittent remarks about how 'you should not be going with such a cold', 'you'll catch flu' and 'you'll be sorry', all uttered out of concern, interspersed with the vocal and physical reactions to the play, such as 'ooh!' and 'YES!!' as clenched fists punched the air – all of which I find rather amusing, how Derek can get so involved with a cricket match which, after all, is only on television. In a rather superior manner, I muttered that I could not see how anyone could get so excited over such a slow game. The reply which came, and I must admit was well deserved, was that Derek could not see how anyone could want to go searching for dung pits on their day off – each to their own. With scores even we sat and watched the news followed by the weather forecast, with the presenter enthusing over the chill factor and the probability of snow. With Derek knowing I have an obstinate streak just like my mother, no more was said.

Having arranged to meet Michael at 8 a.m., I woke to the sound of the wind howling, the dark mornings still proving that spring had not yet arrived. Pulling the covers further over my ears, I began to think that maybe Derek had a good point, and I would be much better off staying in bed – but guilt pushed me out of bed and down the cold corridor in search of the calor gas heater in the kitchen to dress by. Now is the time when I remember all those visitors that come in the summer and tell us how lucky we are to live in this rambling old house with no central heating, and, for two pins, I would swap with them quite happily! Vest, knitted tights, hat and gloves – all a must today. Eventually, kitted up and coughing like a good'un, I made my way across to Cheddar to meet Michael.

I have never been an early bird apart from when I was a dairy maid, and must admit that I prefer to work late, but there is something special about seeing the dark clouds scudding across the sky and giving way to the pink hue of the new dawn. Even the dark empty branches swaying in the stormy winds could not spoil the attractiveness of the shining car headlights weaving their way down the winding roads across the Mendips in the distance. As usual Michael was ready on time; a keen naturalist, he is an early morning person, usually having walked the hills watching deer and all manner of wildlife before I have even thought much about getting out of bed. Tall and slim, he is very fit, as he needs to be – for not only is he a badger consultant but a travel writer as well, his latest venture being to do a sponsored cycle across Israel! He has dark black hair and a full beard, and dare I mention a hint of grey coming in true badger style either side of his forehead; but then he is the same age as me. I hasten to add.

With his usual good humour. Michael loaded my gear into his car with a sarcastic remark about how much women always take with them; I, in turn, remarked at my intrigue at his new car with hydraulic suspension – I had never seen one that sat before! We went on to collect another volunteer and made our way towards Dorset. The weather deteriorated and soon a flurry of snowflakes made it necessary to put the windscreen wipers on. I expect it will soon stop, I thought hopefully, and in fact, by the time we arrived at the meeting place with everyone else it had.

Maps were issued and the pairs agreed, and we set off in separate directions, all to meet back for lunch at 12.30. I was with Michael. Most territorial marking is done beside hedgerows so with one of us walking each side we had to walk the perimeters of all the fields around each hedgeline. Within minutes of our starting out, the snow returned with a vengeance. Pulling my scarf further over my face, I called to Michael to say that if the snow continued to lie we would not be able to see any tracks and signs, and he agreed that we would have to give up if it got worse.

Walking together up a lane we came past a dairy farm. Here was an example of bad farming: slurry had been allowed to seep into a large pond and even the dusting of frosty snowflakes failed to hide the dead black fingers of dying trees that surrounded this area. Pollution was killing not only the pond life and the surrounding rhines (the waterways that divide the fields), but hedgerows and habitats too. Even if steps were taken to stop this contamination, it would be years before the natural balance could be reinstated. Belonging as I do to the farming fraternity, there are times when I feel ashamed of the uncaring attitude of the minority. Thank goodness it is the minority, but they are the ones that create the bad press; and sadly the media believe that what is true of them is true of most farmers.

Moving past and arriving further upfield, we went away from the road and followed the hedgeline, talking occasionally when a badger path was seen going through the hedge and excitedly delving into discovered dung pits looking for the coloured pellets

– if only Derek could see me now! The snow had stopped and the sun shone weakly, but it offered no warmth against the biting wind that was still blowing.

'Oh!' said Michael, from the other side of the hedge, 'I've found one of your friends.'

'Not a badger?' I said incredulously.

'No,' said Michael, 'One of these' – and a hand appeared through the hedge clutching a rook, chilled and hungry and very close to death. Michael has, in the past, brought different animals in distress to us and obviously thought I had come prepared for every eventuality. Warmth was the only thing that could possibly save the rook so the easiest thing was to shove it up my jumper under my coat, and we continued our searching with me clutching 'my bump'.

'Oh!' said Michael in a serious voice, 'here's another one.' I groaned; dedication sometimes goes too far, and the thought of having another rook shoved up my jumper was not a pleasant one. Michael's smiling face appeared through the hedge – 'Only joking!' I poked my tongue out at him.

I had warmed up considerably with all the walking and was beginning to enjoy a morning's freedom away from the commitment of the farm. It is so rare for me to get the chance to walk these days. Intent with looking along the hedgerow and chatting to Michael, I had completely forgotten the rook as it had been so still. The warmth of my body was working and slowly he had regained consciousness; probably being surprised at his unusual surroundings, he suddenly uttered a loud cawing noise. Much to the amusement of Michael, I let out a tremendous scream before I had even had time to register where the noise had come from, other than from somewhere very close. The wretched bird had given me such a shock I almost toyed with the idea of evicting it straightaway. However, it seemed to settle and we carried on with Michael trying his best to hide his mirth.

The time seemed to fly by and soon it was time to go back for lunch and sustenance. Luckily the lady of the house where we had lunch was quite happy to keep the rook in a box with a hot water bottle for the afternoon, so in the second session I found it easier to move, especially when it came to climbing over fences. On one of the hills the badgers had dug their setts in some chalk and the white spoil heaps were visible for a long way. The afternoon passed very pleasantly; the wind had dropped and I was feeling much better in myself.

Travelling down the hedge on the opposite side of the field where we had found the rook, Michael pointed out a buzzard wheeling in the sky, looking for a meal. Buzzards have become a more common sight as the numbers have increased due to the reduction in persecution. Gamekeepers decimated the species at the beginning of the twentieth century but numbers recovered once keepering was greatly reduced after the Second World War. They were to be hit again in the 1950s with the introduction of myxomatosis into our rabbit population, thus destroying their main source of food. Sadly, we now have a new disease that is affecting wild rabbits. Time alone will tell if these beautiful birds are to be once again threatened by a natural calamity.

It always amazes me to see such a large bird glide so effortlessly as it circles, catching the invisible thermals in the sky. The broad wings, held rigid as the tips fan the air, cause it to soar so high that it was easier to hear its mewing call than actually to keep it in sight. All very well, I thought, trying to help wildlife as I had that morning in reviving the rook, but had I inadvertently robbed this buzzard of the meal that he now needed?

Michael asked me to walk up the middle of the field as he mapped out the coloured pellet findings, as the field seemed very large, and he thought that a hedge had been scrubbed out where some pylons crossed. Just as he had supposed, I found a line of dung pits heavily marking the boundary of a territory. The badgers had obviously used the hedge as a boundary and that boundary remained, despite the fact that the hedge was no longer there. Badgers scent-mark their paths and will use exactly the same paths year in and year out. In a field that a badger path crosses, even if it is ploughed up, the path will reappear as the badgers wear down a fresh path in exactly the same place. Looking at the map that Michael had marked in, it was quite fascinating to see how the territories appeared; and of course, however many territories the road crossed, the same number of underpasses would be created when the new road was built.

We were on the last field boundary and making our way back to the car, Michael on the inside of the field while I was walking along the road; as usual we chatted to each other whilst intently looking on the ground for signs. In the distance, I saw a middle-aged lady walking her collie dog coming towards me on the same side of the road. Both sides of the road were lined with quite high hedges and the road was fairly narrow. Slowly, as we came towards each other, she seemed apprehensive and gradually moved further over to the other side of the road the nearer she came to me. She seemed concerned about my presence. As we drew alongside each other, I greeted her with 'Good afternoon', to which she nodded sharply and hurried past. I shook my head and thought that something must have upset her. In that split second she laughed, came back and touched my arm. 'I'm so sorry I ignored you, but I was watching you walk up the road talking to the hedge, and I did not realize you were talking to someone else on the other side – and I must admit, I had grave doubts as to your stability!' We all laughed. Derek, I thought, is obviously not the only one to think I'm mad.

A very contented Pauline went home, head cold much better, having enjoyed a day in the countryside, and complete with rook and hot water bottle cradled on my lap. Sorry – just my kind of day!

Somerset has got to be the county to live in if you are a keen cricketer, because it is home to the willow tree from which cricket

bats are made. Nearly all our fields are surrounded by rhines and often have small ponds in the corner where fields join, just the wet conditions that willows love.

John Beck is a member of the East Huntspill Cricket Team. Although he is younger than Derek, he is very gentlemanly in his manner, making a point of greeting you at a function and kissing the hands of the ladies in farewell at the end of the evening! I had fallen from favour with John, who is a lovely cheery fellow and loves to put on voices when phoning through to people. He is a builder by trade (and a very good one too). On one occasion a few days earlier he had telephoned through to speak to Derek and I had answered. After carrying on a conversation that was absolutely nothing to do with what he wanted, he finally said, 'You don't know who you are talking to, do you?' I had to admit I didn't.

'It's one of the cricket team,' he teased, 'the good-looking one!' Unfortunately I still had no idea. 'You know, the builder', he went on – my mind was blank. 'Oh! come on Pauline,' he groaned, beginning to sound hurt, 'you must recognize me from the description!' Luckily at this point, Derek arrived and I hurriedly put him on the phone – John Beck, I'm sorry!

It was John who went down to the cricket field early one Saturday, to make sure that all was ready for the afternoon match. Often the grass in the outfield has to be cut. On arriving, he noticed that something was caught in the cricket nets; closer inspection revealed it to be a tawny owl. Luckily she had not been there too long, but she was obviously hungry and looking very dishevelled. Very carefully, John released her from the tangled nylon strands and, covering her in a towel, travelled the two miles to our centre to see if we could do anything for her. She was placed in a pen with heat to help her recover from the stress, her large black eyes inquisitive as to her surroundings. Her large clawed feet were spread stoutly on the tree stump in her pen, and you could see the legs softly covered in pale feathers giving the appearance of baggy pants. Her body feathers were ruffled but even so the beautiful colouring of brown, black, buff and chestnut plumage still made her majestic in appearance. If she sat in the fork of a tree, her wonderful colouring would be complete camouflage against the bark of her daytime roost. She would need to be safe because, if sighted during the day, groups of birds would mob her in order to drive her away and disturb her daytime resting period. With her body totally still, she turned her head to listen to any unusual sound, slowly opening and closing the lids of her eyes independently, thus giving the impression of winking. Owls have very large eyes so that they can see in poor light. They are forward-facing like human eyes but, unlike us, owls are unable to move their eyes from side to side. In order to overcome this, they are able to swivel their head to right and left over their shoulders, so that they can literally see everything that is going on behind them as well as in front without moving their body. (Quite useful as a human quality, I should imagine, especially when driving a car with argumentative children in the back!)

Luckily, she had not broken any bones and appeared just hungry and tired, so she was left in peace to recover. We kept her for a few days to make sure she was eating properly. However, one of our biggest problems is that we do not have large aviary facilities to be able to assess the condition of a bird properly. On the occasions that we had the owl out in the hospital room she appeared to fly well but was still fairly quiet, so as she was eating well, we thought time would heal.

The following Monday turned out to be a very hectic day. Derek was out delivering leaflets to venues to advertise our centre and, as usual, one thing had led to another through the day and I was way behind with my work. About 5 p.m. I prepared a salad thinking that it would be ready no matter what time we were going to eat.

Derek came home about an hour later and we had a cup of tea together before starting work again. 'When are we eating?' Derek asked. I told him about the salad but said that I would have mine later. If I have a lot of work to do in the evening, I can keep going as long as I don't eat, but once I stop to eat a meal, I find it very difficult to get going again – must be my age! Derek was not feeling all that hungry, so he said he would wait and have his with me. By 10 p.m. the pangs of hunger were showing as pain on his face, so I darted through to our store to get a couple of potatoes to do as jackets quickly in the microwave. Our hospital room backs on to the store and as I went in to get the potatoes, I could hear the tawny owl fluttering in her pen. It sounded as if she was ready to go, and the constant battering of her wings against the sides of the pen could possibly damage her feathers. Returning to my long-suffering husband in the kitchen, I broached the subject. 'You don't think', I started with pleading eyes, 'that we could just pop that tawny owl back to the cricket field as it sounds as if she is ready to go – it would be lovely to see her go, and then we could sit down and have our tea?'

Placing the newspaper to one side, he sighed and got up. 'You and your animals!' Five minutes later found us sitting in the car, Derek driving, and me with the owl wrapped in a towel ready for release. The road from the village leading to the cricket field is very small and we slowly made our way to the metal gate at the entrance. There were no lights other than the headlights of the car, but it was a moonlit night and we could see quite well. I jumped at an unusual sound: 'What was that?' I asked, looking to see if Derek had heard it too. 'It was my stomach rumbling', was his serious reply. 'Never mind,' I said, trying to keep the conversation light, 'I'll place her on the gate and we can go home.' Gently holding her so that she could grip the post by the gate, I slowly took away the towel and we stood and waited. These are usually times that we savour, as to return an animal or bird back to the wild really gives you a lift. Not this time. The tawny owl went to fly but obviously there must still have been some bruising to her wings; she was not fit enough to gain height and she drifted down into the grass. Anxious to recapture her and without thinking it out

too well, Derek made a dive for her, but she took off once more covering just a short distance which ended with a *plop*! The tawny had managed to reach the side of the field and was floating in the middle of a pond. Uttering a word under his breath, Derek could see that tea was going to be even later. 'Er, – you couldn't just pop back home,' I asked sweetly, 'and get some nets and a couple of torches, could you?'

The car disappeared back up the lane, and I tried desperately to see where she was, hoping that her feathers would not soak up the water too fast. Actually she had managed to reach a branch in the middle of the pond and was sitting quite happily out of the water. Minutes passed and very soon I heard the car returning. 'Can you see her?' Derek asked as he got out of the car. There you see, I thought, he is concerned.

'Because if she's drowned, we can go home!'

'No,' I replied, 'She's in the centre – oh, did you only bring one net and torch?'

'I suppose you want me to go back and get another,' Derek said curtly. 'No,' I replied brightly, 'I'm sure we'll manage.' But of course each time we went one side of the pond, the owl moved just far enough to the other side to be out of our reach.

Determination wins the day and eventually, covered in briars and nettle rash, two soldiers scrabbled out of the thicket complete with sopping wet owl.

Half past twelve that night found me putting the finishing touches to a delicious salad and a husband sat with a hairdryer warming the tawny up – he does care for animals really.

From all our mistakes we learn. That owl, once it had got over the shock, had a ring put on its leg for identity and was taken to the RSPCA Wildlife Unit near Taunton to be put into a large aviary to regain muscle condition. Only then, when fully fit, was she returned to us and we finally released her properly. This is the procedure that we now follow. One day we may have our own aviary facilities to avoid the stress of the transportation.

To see an owl flying free is fantastic. Yes, when we have them in as casualties, it is easy to understand people's longing to own them as pets but how much more rewarding it is to see them in their natural environment and perhaps, by being wildlife volunteers, to help create or protect their habitat.

I have never fully understood the comradeship of the cricket team as I have always thought that as a team you pulled together and would be tactful about any unfortunate occurrences that usually a member would wish to forget. This is not so with the East Huntspill cricket team, who seem to delight in any information obtained to the detriment of another member – but in a light-hearted manner, of course. Probably, this is the main reason for one of the awards given each season at the annual dinner. This special award is for the player who has done the most to obtain the much valued title of Idiot of the Year!

Sadly, Derek has won this award on two occasions. He is the kit manager of the club and takes sole responsibility for the kit bag and the condition of equipment. Should they need new bats, balls or otherwise, it is up to him to make the committee aware of this need and thus get permission to purchase the new equipment required. The first year of his accolade, he had noticed that they were soon going to need a new kit bag as the stitching had gone on the old one; it had also been remarked that a few pairs of leg pads were required. Making a mental note of this, Derek thought he would bring this up at the next committee meeting. Prior to this meeting Derek missed playing for a couple of weeks and the kit went to another player to look after; on his return to playing for the team the kit was given back to Derek to keep during the week, and this he went on to do for the next three weeks before the committee meeting.

The committee meeting is held at the local pub, the Basonbridge, which usually means that there is a good turn-out. Warwick is the chairman and has been for yonks, probably because he's too big to argue with. A founder member, he has ruled the team with determination and enthusiasm – on and off the pitch, although he does not always abide by the rules that he himself instigates! Paul Gass (the life-saver) is ever the voice to be heard; he does a lot to organize functions for fundraising and at the same time enjoys himself so much to the full that we all suffer from his singing as a result of complete inebriation. All the committee members make sure not to give Warwick an easy ride on controlling the matters in hand, much to his despair: he always has one eye on the clock as to when the food will be ready. Larry, a more studious member of the group, is the main organizer of all the general knowledge quiz evenings; his memory of facts (especially about the Eurovision Song Contest) amazes all. He is even a good guitar player but has often had to abandon a performance because of the continual barracking from the rest of the team with such kind remarks that I would not

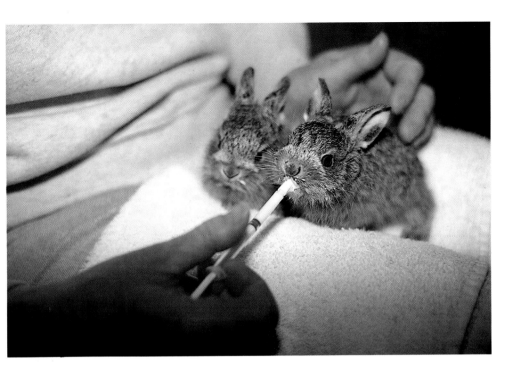

Two rescued baby leverets, a little brother and sister – the female (*below*) survived and was later released, as seen on ITV's Animal Country

Daisy the cat enjoys the tortoises' infra red lamp

This pretty roebuck deer was one of the all too frequent road casualties

Debbie with a couple of foxy friends, Amber and Misty

Up comes Mr Mole
– an unusual view as
he was more often
seen disappearing
downwards!

Murray as a (greedy)
pup

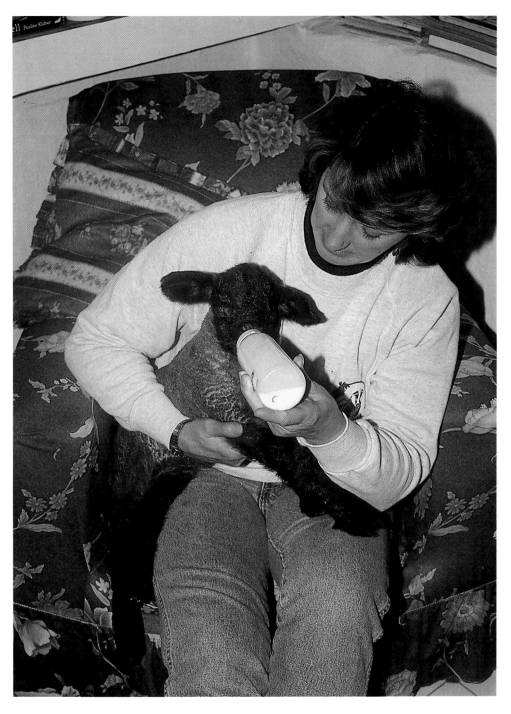

Pauline feeding Ethel the lamb

Dot the red deer is always keen on seeing if there are any titbits in the coffee room . . .

. . . *opposite*, she is delighted to share a cuppa with Pauline

A long-term resident Sage the barn owl shows off for the camera

Muscovy mum with ducklings

like to repeat. Mike Bell with his dry wit, Ian and Russell, they were all sitting around the table when it came to the time for the kit manager's report.

'Anything to report, Derek?' asked Warwick, conscious that the food should now be ready and if left much longer would be ruined. He glanced at his watch. 'Well, there were just a couple of things,' said Derek.

All eyes turned to face him.

'We do seem to need a new kit bag,' said Derek. A ripple of laughter broke out.

'New kit bag?' asked Warwick, no longer worried about the food because he had a suspicion that Derek was about to make a crass statement.

'Well yes,' said Derek. 'The stitching has gone and one of the straps has nearly broken and . . .' Everyone was watching, willing him to carry on, and he wondered just what was so amusing. Changing tack he then said, 'and of course, there's the leg pads . . .'

Raucous laughter broke out. 'Well they're very tatty and . . . just what is so funny?' Derek said. By this time Paul Gass had practically disappeared under the table, Mike Bell was in tears, and Warwick, pulling himself to his full height, walked over to Derek and said, 'You have been playing for the past three weeks, Derek, haven't you?'

'Yes', said Derek – he really couldn't think what he had said that was so funny.

'Carried the kit bag out to the field and back to the car each time?' asked Warwick.

The meeting collapsed. Russell, with great aplomb, explained to Derek that they had been aware of needing a new kit bag, and even the leg pads, and during the period Derek had not played they had decided to go ahead and purchase new leg pads which had been put in a new kit bag which for the last three weeks Derek had been carrying to each match. They had got him – game, set and match!

The second year of obtaining this award was the year of the balls! Just before the start of the season, Derek ordered some new cricket balls from a firm who required payment with the order. This was then discussed at a committee meeting and a cheque issued. Through no fault of his own, the cricket balls were lost in the post and Derek had to report this occurrence to the team as well as filling in the lengthy claim forms obtained from the Post Office. Telephone calls were made, enquiries were all carried out officially in the hope of tracking down these balls. Our local postman, aware of the situation, would shake any suitable parcel that he delivered, teasing Derek that it might be his balls! The innuendoes were numerous and funny the first few times, but we eventually dreaded getting anything that was roughly the right size! Of course, the team-mates had a field day, ragging Derek as to the carelessness of losing his balls etc., etc. In fact they never did turn up and replacements were sent.

Derek had an inkling that this episode may have placed him in the running for the award but he managed to make himself a clear candidate in the latter part of the season, the winter, when they all meet for indoor net practice. That year everyone was travelling to Taunton which for most of them was a 30-minute run. They were hiring the nets at the County Ground for an hour. The number of players that turned up varied from one week to the next, but this particular week they had a really good turn-out and Derek said everyone was catching up on local gossip as they donned their pads ready to practise. Slowly the lads accumulated on the side of the nets and started to delve into the kit bag that Derek had brought down. Unfortunately, no matter how deep they delved, there was not a single ball to be found – Derek had forgotten to bring them with him. You cannot, by the way, play cricket without a ball, even I know that. He was not what you would call a popular man that day, and that certainly sealed his fate as winner of the award for that year.

The award, by the way, is usually something atrocious such as a broken trophy or whatever, but there was a twist to the award that Derek received the second time. When we first started our open farm, we were not too sure about the buying of giftware for the shop, so we talked to someone in a similar business who advised that visitors loved to buy dog ornaments. We now realize that it was either false information or he truly had different visitors from us, as we purchased all these dog ornaments from a firm and it took all of three years to clear the stock. 'The biggest mistake you can make', someone said at a trade fair, 'is to buy things that you like, because it is the gaudy stuff that will sell.' Maybe Derek had this in mind when he purchased this particular line for our shop, or maybe it was because the representative was a very attractive lady, but he ordered some hideous crockery with flowers and dogs painted on it. To be fair most of it did sell, but there were a few pieces that really were horrendous which stayed and stayed. Eventually we were down to the last plate: cream china with a bulldog square in the middle and roses up the side – just the sort of thing that everyone would love. The time came for a function in aid of the cricket club and all the members had to donate a raffle prize; desperate to get rid of it, one of the prizes that Derek so thoughtfully gave was this dreadful plate.

The big draw took place at the end of the evening, and with great amusement to all, Warwick was the lucky winner of the plate. Surprisingly, he was not keen to keep this acquisition and when he had the opportunity of giving it away, when his mother asked him to donate a prize for the tombola at a Conservative evening, Warwick jumped at the chance. The event was quite a large one and was very well attended, and with all the local support the tombola boasted many prizes. These were all on display; there were so many that they had been colour-coded, so there was a pink raffle prize stand, a yellow stand, and so on. Warwick, dutifully attending the social, chanced his luck on the tombola. He pulled out his tickets: lo and behold, he had a winning pink ticket. The lady in charge directed him over to the table holding the pink ticket prizes and he scanned for his number. He could not believe it: he found the number proudly stuck to the plate that he had donated. Warwick had yet again won this wonderful plate!

When the nominations are discussed for all the awards, Warwick, as chairman, is involved, and on hearing that Derek was to win the Idiot of the Year Award, he said he had exactly the right thing to give him as a prize. Yes, we do still have it and if you know of anyone who would like a cream plate with a bulldog on the front and roses round the sides . . .

There was, dare I say, even a third year when Derek seemed to be heading for this award yet again, but luckily someone else in the team committed an even worse crime and, by the skin of his teeth, Derek managed to get away with it.

Most years the cricket team try to go away on tour and, this particular year, they planned to go to Jersey. Derek has many fond memories of Jersey as he holidayed there as a teenager, and the family endured details of this holiday every time Bergerac came on television. Now he was going to get the chance to visit again.

The one thing about being open to the public is that, in the summer, you are very busy and usually do not get the chance to do the things that most tourists do. Derek has always enjoyed the heat of the summer and, if there is one thing he misses, it is the chance to go swimming in the sea. Booked to join the team, Derek was counting the days until his break of cricket, sea and sun, and as the time drew near the weather was beautiful. We were enjoying a really warm spell. At the same time, I had been hand-rearing two badger cubs, Bill and Boris, in the kitchen with all the associated fun of trying to stop them destroying the furniture and carpet. Now weaned, they had moved out of the kitchen and had joined some other badger cubs in the casualty pens ready to form a social group, prior to release. I was hoping, with a little more time on my hands, to do some decorating while Derek was away. I planned to paint the kitchen. With Derek out of the way, I could scrap doing meals, turn the room upside-down and get on with it!

The team was flying from Bristol Airport on the Friday at 10 a.m., arriving in Jersey in time to settle in and then play an evening game. Saturday was to be a free day and Sunday was an all-day match. They were due to return on the 11 a.m. flight on Monday, arriving in Bristol Airport at 12 noon. The team had arranged lifts to the airport on the Friday but Derek asked me if I could be one of the pick-up cars on the Monday to bring them home, which was fine by me. Thursday evening was spent busily checking that all Derek's kit was ready, looking out the clothes he would need, and remembering with extra care to pack his reading glasses as he now finds reading such things as menus and posters difficult without them. We were so busy that we failed to notice the weather report for the weekend, which showed a cold front moving towards the southern part of England bringing rain and mist.

The day dawned bright on Friday morning with no hint of the weather to come, and the car came to collect Derek for the grand tour. Although we like to take holidays together, it is easier in the summer for one to stay behind. We both work so hard that we really need the rest when we can get it, so I was pleased to see Derek go off for a nice relaxed couple of days away from all the worries.

I charged upstairs to the kitchen; without further ado, the pictures came down and the ornaments off the shelves, and with the radio blaring, I set to washing the paintwork ready to start the decorating. Crawling around on my hands and knees, I began to see just how much damage had been done to the carpet by the badger cubs during their stay and decided that maybe a change-round of furniture would hide a few details. Looking at the clock, I noticed it was nearly 11 a.m. Time for coffee – Derek must be just arriving in Jersey by now, I thought. Sitting reading the newspaper having my coffee, I was unaware that Derek was also sitting reading the newspaper – in fog-bound Bristol Airport.

Pleased with my efforts so far, I went downstairs to collect fresh paint and brushes ready to start painting the walls. Going back upstairs, I stopped: I could hear voices that I recognized coming from the kitchen in the tearooms below. It was some relatives who were calling in on the off-chance that I would be there – they hadn't seen me for years. Placing the paint pots and brushes in our private kitchen, and glancing around at the room which looked like a bomb had hit it, I decided to keep them downstairs. It was lovely to see them but my day was slipping away – and I had so hoped to get my kitchen painted. Luckily they were going on to Mum and Dad for lunch so at least I would have the afternoon.

Seeing them off (which did not take long as it was pouring with rain), I turned to go back indoors only to be met by Mandy, our animal care supervisor, to say we were nearly out of dog food and it was Saturday tomorrow, when our suppliers would be closed. The best-laid plans of mice and men – chocolate bar in hand for lunch, I drove to Bridgwater for dog food. At least, as it was Mandy's fault that she had not realized we were low on dog food, I had twisted her arm to do the milking so I could get on with the painting once I got back. And surprise, surprise, I did – well, I was about half-way round the kitchen with emulsion by the early evening when Derek rang to say they had arrived. The airport had remained fog-bound and eventually they were all taken by coach to Exeter Airport and had flown from there. The hotel, when they arrived, didn't quite live up to their expectations but at least it was comfortable.

On arrival they sorted out their rooms and Derek was given the key for his room, which he was sharing with Paul Gass. Before he went up to the room, Derek stayed and chatted with the others. It looked as though the evening match was going to be cancelled as it was pouring with rain and it was really quite cold. Paul wanted to go up to the room and get unpacked so he called across to Derek, asking what number room they were in. Glancing at the key fob Derek called out '84' and carried on talking – with the free day the next day there was much discussion as to where to visit. Some half an hour later Paul reappeared, suitcase still in hand, having visited every floor in the hotel and unable to find an

84. On closer inspection, and with his glasses on, Derek was able to see that the key fob was actually number 34. Paul, refraining from commenting, went in search of room 34.

'Paul's got over it now,' said Derek when he phoned me; and it appeared that an evening in the bar was in order seeing as there was to be no match. 'How's the decorating going?' he enquired. 'Slow but sure,' I replied, telling him of all my interruptions; 'Still another couple of hours and the one coat will be done.' Promising to ring the next evening, Derek went off to the bar and I picked up my paint brush. I was soon to be interrupted yet again by a telephone call from a lady at Glastonbury who had an injured bat in her garden. She couldn't possibly pick it up but she had put a box over it and would I please come and get it? I explained that I would be unable to get to her until after I had shut up the chickens, which in the summer can be quite late; given the half-hour journey, it would be about 11 p.m. That was all right, she would wait up for me.

Climbing over the fences and shutting all the chicken-house doors, I worked out that by the time I got back it would be about midnight, just another hour or so would see the end of painting the first coat. Second coat put on during Saturday, gloss on Sunday, yes I could still be done by Monday before Derek got back. Driving to Glastonbury, I had a chance to listen to some tapes. I often find driving quite relaxing. Mrs Jarrold's house was easy to find and, as she had promised, the outside light left switched on told me which one of the terraced houses belonged to her.

So grateful to me for coming so late at night, she took me round to the back garden. There I discovered that the bat in question was well and truly dead! 'I'm sure I saw it move', Mrs Jarrold said apologetically. The only movement that she might have seen would have been involuntary movements of the body as the maggots inside squirmed around – it was as high as a kite! When these incidents occur, it is never a waste of time. In the first place, it was good enough of the person concerned to contact someone to help a wild creature. In so many cases people would not even bother, and I would much rather go out on a wild goose chase than run the risk of an animal being left unattended to die.

I was soon back to finish the painting and as there was no patient to deal with on my return I was able to get stuck in straightaway. It always seems easier to work at night, no interruptions, no telephone ringing!

Saturday for me went off without a hitch, but not for Derek. When he rang in the early evening, he explained that he did not think he was going to be in everybody's good books later on. As Derek had gone down to breakfast in the morning he had passed a notice-board with a poster advertising Bernard Manning at a local night-club. Now Bernard Manning is one of his favourites. Asking at reception where this night-club was, he was told that it was not far away but it was quite a high-class club and they would not allow anyone in unless they were properly dressed, certainly no jeans. Over breakfast, Derek had managed to persuade the rest of the team to go to the night-club that evening but some of them had not brought proper trousers with them, so those who only had jeans went into town to buy some new clothes for the evening out.

On his way down to the telephone to ring me, Derek had just noticed that the poster was for a cabaret starring Bernard Manning that would be on in a fortnight's time; and, as yet, he had not been able to tell most of the team because they had not returned from their shopping trip. Having bought new clothes especially, Derek did not think they would be too pleased!

As it happened, despite Bernard Manning not being on that evening, the team still decided to go to the same night-club. All dressed up they made their way to this posh club and, on arrival, filed through the main entrance, past the bouncers. The last one to go in was Ian, one of the dutiful ones who had had to go shopping to purchase new trousers for this special evening, but unfortunately he was still wearing trainers as he had not brought any shoes with him. The bouncer stopped him and explained that there was no way that Ian was going in if he didn't have proper shoes on. Ian decided to return to the hotel, sure that someone would wonder where he was and come looking for him. No one else in the party noticed that he had been stopped and, once inside, they spotted he was missing, but with their usual caring attitude did not bother to find out where he had gone. So Ian spent a lonely night on his own.

On the Sunday, the only thing that Derek managed to do wrong was to lose his coat somewhere. The match organized for the Sunday turned out to be with the Jersey 1st Team who just about wiped the floor with them as they were way above the level of cricket that East Huntspill would usually play. Still, it was a very enjoyable luncheon and tea, he told me.

Monday arrived in Jersey, another grey and miserable day. In fact the whole weekend had been cold and miserable and Derek certainly had not been for his swim in the sea. Arriving at the airport for the return flight, Derek realized that his return ticket had been in the coat that he had lost and there was a panic situation which was only resolved by paying out a further £15 for the expense of issuing a replacement ticket.

Knowing that their flight was arriving at midday, I left the farm at 11 a.m. to get to Bristol Airport in time. Five minutes after I had left, Derek rang to say that their flight had been delayed indefinitely once again due to fog. This, of course, was too late to tell me. On arriving at the airport, I did the usual thing of drifting around the vicinity of the arrivals lounge; it was only after catching a garbled message on that dreadful tannoy that I asked at Enquiries and was told that Jersey was completely fog-bound and they doubted that there would be any flights out that day. I didn't really mind apart from the wasted journey because I hadn't finished the painting! Meanwhile, the lads back at Jersey started to console themselves with the duty free bar whilst they waited for news. Eventually, because one of the players had to be in Holland the next day, it was arranged for them to go by hovercraft across to Weymouth and then to be picked up by coach and driven for the last lap of the journey, which would take approximately three hours. Being one of the few who had not participated in the duty free, Derek was involved in the rounding-up of the merry men and even in directing to and from the toilet.

A very tired and sad team arrived on home ground at 2.30 in the morning. Derek rang to see if I could pick him up and drop some of the others home. When I answered the phone, he said: 'That was quick, were you still up?' Up? I was still painting!

I don't know why, but once the cricket season starts and Derek is away on Saturday things start to go wrong. Perhaps it is because more people go walking at weekends but it does seem to be a busier time for calls out to injured animals.

Sometimes, you do things without realizing what could be the consequence if it were to go wrong. Early one Saturday morning, I had a telephone call from a vet in Weston, who had a roedeer buck that she was treating. It had been knocked down by a car and the driver had brought it into her surgery. She had stitched the animal up, but there appeared to be no broken bones. At the moment the deer was unconscious, but quite rightly the vet was concerned about it. The accommodation that it was in was a dog pen with the kind of wire netting that a deer could easily catch its legs in and break them. Deer have a very nervous disposition and if this buck came round while still in this restricted area, it might start to thrash around and could soon damage itself quite badly.

We really don't have suitable accommodation for deer and I have not really had any dealings with them other than hand-rearing a fawn, so I advised that she contact the RSPCA but on the understanding that if there was any problem she should come back to me. I rang her after half an hour, having given her time to make arrangements, to make sure that everything was all right. The RSPCA were evidently very busy but expected to pick the deer up by the afternoon. She hoped it would be all right until then. As it was a Saturday, Derek had been busy getting his jobs done so that he could be ready to get down to the cricket field by 1 p.m. It was a fairly quiet day as far as visitors were concerned, so I was hoping to catch up on some book work. With his sports bag packed, Derek came and found me in the office to say he was off and not to expect him back until about 11–11.30 p.m. Not that he would be playing cricket all this time, but it was necessary to discuss the strategy of the game played that afternoon, probably at a local hostelry, and Derek has never been one to appear rude and leave the pub before everyone else!

Within minutes of him driving off in the van, I had another call from the lady vet at Weston. Sounding very distressed, she told me that the RSPCA had just contacted her to say that, due to pressure of calls, they would be unable to collect the deer until the following Monday – an impossible situation. In this day and age, most businesses, no matter who they are, have to run as efficiently as possible with as few staff as possible in order to reduce costs. This is fine when everything goes smoothly, but when a lot of calls come in together, it is often up to the person on duty taking calls to prioritize the call-outs. That person may not have a great deal of knowledge on specific animals, so maybe in assessing which cases were to be dealt with first, they thought that an animal left at a vet's could wait longer than another call-out. In my opinion, on this occasion, they had made the wrong decision. That deer had to be moved as quickly as possible, not only for its own safety but for the safety of the people handling it as well. I told her I would sort something out and contact her within 10 minutes.

Quickly, I telephoned Colin Seddon at the RSPCA Wildlife Unit near us, and with fingers crossed, prayed that he would be there. My luck was in. Colin could not be away from the centre for too long as they were short-staffed, and I had to be back to milk for the visitors in the afternoon, so we arranged between us that I should collect the deer from the vet's, return to our centre with it, and then Colin would drive out and meet me here and take it on to the unit.

'If there is any chance of it coming round from the anaesthetic, then get the vet to top it up with another injection before you leave the surgery, and take care,' said Colin.

Acting quickly, I rang the vet to say we were leaving straightaway and went looking for my mother to accompany me so that there was another pair of hands in the car. Mum, as usual, was pottering around in the garden in her old clothes and red wellies. Sensing my urgency, she gave up on worrying about her appearance and we drove off towards Weston.

My mother is now in her seventies although one would never believe it the way she flits around the place, one minute gardening, the next washing up in the tearoom. In fact both my parents are a tremendous help and we would be lost without them. Dad does reception work some of the time and enjoys tinkering in the workshop but finds it difficult to understand that, with so many of us using things, articles are rarely returned to where they should be; often, father despairs that even a simple job takes ages by the time you've tracked down the tool required (and then you're lucky if you've managed to find it!). Dad's opening sentence on coming into the room is 'You haven't seen the so-and-so, have you?' I had not realized how much this affected him until recently, when Derek and I were lucky enough to go abroad for a summer holiday. On our return, the first thing that Dad said when he saw us was 'You didn't take the hacksaw away on holiday with you, did you? I've looked everywhere for it and I can't find it.' What a welcome home!

Anyway, both Mum and I quite enjoyed the drive over to the vet's because, although she is usually around the farm, actually to hold a conversation without being interrupted is practically impossible. So we had a good natter and before we knew it we had arrived at Weston. The vet was relieved to see us, as she thought the deer was beginning to come round. 'Could you dose him up with some more anaesthetic', I gaily asked, 'to keep him sedated while we move him?'

'I can't do that,' the vet said, 'he's not under anaesthetic, it is only shock that is causing him to be unconscious. If I give him anaesthetic on top we could lose him. I'll hobble him for you if you like.' I would have preferred the anaesthetic. By hobbling, you tie the ankles of the animal together, front legs together and back legs together. In domestic animals this would disable them, but I had my doubts with a deer.

She took me through to where the deer was. Mum had stayed in the car. I could see what the vet meant by the unsuitable accommodation as the buck was at least a couple of years old and was lying sleeping in a large cage suitable for a very large dog. He would not have had head room, let alone anything else, if he came to. I was also aware of the twitching of his reflexes, which made me think that the quicker we got this over, the better.

Having hobbled his legs, we both carried him carefully out to the car and lay him gently on the back seat. It seemed pitiful to see such a beautiful wild creature so incapacitated. His summer coat was a lovely sandy red and his antlers, stark and fully formed, showed that he was at least two years old. Come October they would be shed and fresh ones grown again by March, covered in a fine furry skin called velvet. His exquisitely fine legs were draped over the seat. They, with the fine shiny black hooves, belied the tremendous speeds, in leaps and bounds, that the spindly legs are capable of. Roedeer are said to be able to jump up to 16 metres (17 yards) in a single spring.

Wishing us luck, the vet waved goodbye, quite relieved that her problem was now ours! My mother was slowly stroking the deer's face and murmuring words of consolation to it; she was completely unaware of the kind of situation we would have on our hands if the buck woke up! I thought it best not to enlighten her, but was mentally working out a strategy for if the worst came to the worst as I swung the car on to the motorway. Half an hour and we would be home – just stay unconscious for another forty minutes, I prayed. It did not look as though it was going to be just half an hour as the car slowed and I joined an endless line of traffic, all three lanes of the motorway full and speeds down to 30 miles an hour. Of course, it was Saturday – in the middle of the summer season, everyone was going on holiday. A slight movement in the back was enough to make me decide to use the hard shoulder, and with hazard lights flashing I was able to make better time. Overtaking the queues of traffic on the emergency lane, at that particular moment I was more afraid of a thrashing deer than a flashing policeman!

With heart in mouth and clammy hands, I made it back to the farm just as Colin was arriving in the RSPCA hospital van. He had a young girl with him and swiftly we transferred the deer to the van. His eyes widened as I told him that the deer was not under anaesthetic, and he immediately told the girl to get in the back with the deer and he would get going as quickly as he could. His last instructions to the girl as she climbed into the back were: 'If the deer comes round, throw the whole of your body on top of it and bang the side of the van and I will stop and come and help you.' As they drove off, I had this wonderful mental picture of what could have happened on the way back from Weston if the deer had come round, and the thought of my mother stretched out on top of the deer complete with her red wellie boots did not bear thinking about!

Sadly, many deer are knocked down on the road, and it all happens so quickly that usually the deer finds the strength to get away from the scene only to die later. For those who have had the pleasure of seeing these lovely secretive animals, especially at dawn with the mist still rising, it is a sight they will never forget.

Certainly I remember our own roedeer kid that we reared some years ago. Roedeer are similar to badgers in that they have delayed implantation; although the mating is carried out in the period July to August (called the rut) the blastocyst does not implant until late December or early January so that the kids are usually born between mid-May and mid-June. Deer have their young and often leave them in the long grass for periods of time while they graze, sometimes quite a long way away from them. If they have more than one, and twins are quite usual, the young will split up and wait for the mother to return. This is so that if they are predated, hopefully only one will be killed. It is when they are lying up in this way that the general public, while they are out walking, sometimes find them and think that they are orphans. Unless they seem stressed in any way, they really are best left alone and the mother will return. In a way, it is surprising that more are not found as the distribution of deer in Britain is quite extensive. In fact, over 15,000 roedeer are culled annually to prevent numbers increasing to such an extent that they would cause a lot of damage to trees and habitats. How finely balanced everything has to be.

Bramble, our roedeer kid, we were able to return to the wild. I must admit that it was one of the hardest things I had to do when he went to join others of his own kind, but it was the best for him and I hope he survived.

At the moment we are home to Dot, a young red deer hind. She was another example of a young deer being picked up by people thinking she was orphaned. They took her to a couple very proficient in wildlife care, a postman and his wife, and Dot was reared by them. Unfortunately, because she never saw any of her own kind, she has grown up with the idea that she is a human being. Francesca, the lady who reared her, contacted us when Dot was six months old to see if we could take her on. Fran knew that Dot needed to be near people and wanted her to go somewhere where she would be shown to the public as an educational aid to explain why you must leave young deer alone.

Mandy, our animal supervisor, came out with me when I went to have a look at Dot. I wanted to make sure that Dot was so imprinted that she would be able to cope with being moved to a strange environment without reverting to being wild and running madly off into the sunset.

Francesca had given me instructions to find their cottage, and it was a good job they were detailed as we wound our way through the hills at the foot of Exmoor, seemingly miles and miles away from anywhere. We eventually arrived at the cottage, and Francesca came out to greet us with both her boys, home from school, arguing over where to dig a hole in the garden. Both Fran and her husband have cared for wildlife in the past and we chatted easily, exchanging views on caring, as Francesca guided us down the garden path to a paddock at the side of the house.

She did not need to call Dot because Dot had already spotted us. Bounding over towards us at an incredible speed, she came to an abrupt stop just as you felt that impact was imminent. She was much larger than I had imagined, although still elegantly graceful despite being waist-height. There wasn't an ounce of shyness – indeed, Dot could see no reason why she could not come into the house with us for a cup of coffee!

Deciding to risk it, I found myself once again arranging to move a deer, but this time in the van, and Francesca offered to come as well to quieten her down. Dot was still having a bottle of milk twice a day and we decided that when she came to the farm, only Mandy would feed her to get Dot to recognize Mandy as her new surrogate mother, having lost contact with Francesca.

The day arrived for collecting her and it went as smoothly as it could have done. Placing straw in the van for Dot, Francesca climbed in and Dot followed without even a word of encouragement. Driving very carefully, I was aware that travelling was not one of Dot's previous experiences and I must admit there was (once again) just a fleeting thought of a thrashing deer in the back. Francesca's mind was running along the same lines, as she commented that if anything went wrong and Dot broke one of her legs, Francesca would want her put down. Whether or not this was understood by Dot I'm not sure, but she soon lay down and gazed contentedly out of the window.

Arriving at the farm, it seemed a far cry from her original home in the peace and quiet of the hills; for here there is much movement, the sounds of different animals and, in the distance, the roar of the motorway. Quietly Dot was guided into a large pen. It had windows so that she could see her outside surroundings but we had barred them so that she could not jump at them and break the glass. I had thought that we could put her with a goat in the hope that she would pal up with it and then the two of them could graze alongside in the nearby orchard.

Dot was not amused by this arrangement! It was quite evident from the sheer disgust on her face that there was no way that an affinity between them was ever going to be struck, and we decided to keep her on her own. Francesca was very good and stayed for a couple of hours to make sure that Dot settled; she could have been easily dismayed at the nonchalant attitude Dot had to her new surroundings, but was pleased that she seemed settled. I said I would ring her and let her know how Dot got on. Francesca put on a very brave face as she and her husband made their way to the gate, but the final exit was too much as she sobbed against her husband at leaving Dot behind.

I knew exactly how she felt and promised that if anything went wrong and Dot seemed unhappy I would let her know and she could take her back. Her husband led her to the car and they were gone.

Going back to check on Dot, I silently hoped that we had done the right thing. Would she accept us as her home? I knew that if she wandered off, with the speeds that deer can reach the motorway was within easy reach, and we do have neighbours that shoot. Nothing ventured, nothing gained, but that didn't stop me worrying.

Mandy gave Dot her bottle twice a day and all the girls working here were fascinated by her. As Dot took her bottle, the scent glands by her eyes opened and were clearly visible. These are the glands that deer use to mark their territory, often giving the impression that they are poking their eyes with the stems of the bushes.

After keeping her enclosed for two weeks, so that she accepted the pen as her home, we started to allow her out for half an hour at a time and she followed Mandy around as good as gold. The problem was when to take the final step and allow her the freedom to come and go.

The problem resolved itself one day, when the girls all did their jobs early so they could do some surveying for badgers at a local village. Whoever fed Dot last did not shut the door properly and unbeknown to us she found her way to the orchard. It was the same day that we had paid a young lad to come and chainsaw some wood from the woodpile in the orchard ready for our open fires in the farmhouse. Half-way through the morning, he came round to the office and asked if it was possible to take the deer in as she kept nudging his elbow while he was trying to cut the wood – which with a chainsaw was a bit dangerous really! We decided there and then that if she was that bomb-proof we could leave her out during the day.

Dot now wanders around all through the day, chasing after one of the girls or nosing in the dairy to see if there is anything left lying around to eat. The hardest part is keeping her out of the tearoom. As you can imagine she is a favourite with the visitors but, as with many deer, she finds roses, hedges and the willow trees very attractive. Many of our bushes have frayed branches where they have been chewed by Dot, as deer do not have top teeth and they tear the greenery as they eat. She is, therefore, not so popular with Reg the gardener.

Somerset may be the home of the willow trees, which are sometimes grown for cricket bats, but not at our home because Dot has eaten them – good for her!

4

Media

When we entered the world of tourism and opened our farm
to the public, little did we realize the fun that was to be
in store!

Slowly over the years, we have changed to being a rescue
centre for badgers and many kinds of wild creatures that find
their way to us. Every day, newspapers try to run at least
one animal story in their publications, so the reporters are
kept busy looking for new stories. If news is hard to find,
they start ringing round the different animal centres, asking if
there is anything new and unusual that has arrived and they
will then do a little article on them. Just before Christmas one
year, a reporter contacted me, looking for a story to push out
in the nationals. It was winter and the one animal that most
wildlife centres would be looking after would be hedgehogs, the
ones that are too small to hibernate through the winter, which
are taken in and looked after until the spring, when they are
released again. Just about every paper had featured a story on a

hedgehog and they were looking for something different to write a story about.

'Anything new?' asked Alan, when he got through to me.

'It's really been very quiet,' I answered, 'you've featured the hedgehogs, and everything else that we have in is fairly mundane and there is no background story that would interest you for publishing.'

'Oh,' said Alan, disappointed.

'I'm sorry,' I replied, 'but if I told you anything different, it wouldn't be the truth.'

'Oh!' said Alan, enthusiasm back in his voice, 'it doesn't have to be the truth, just give me something and I'll build on it!'

This conversation just about sums up newspapers in general – but they do help us with publicity, so when we can, we help. But we now know that whatever we read in a paper has to be taken with a pinch of salt. What's more, when the photographers come to take pictures of you with the animal, they always want you or the animal in the most impossible positions. There is one photographer in particular who will talk incessantly, spouting instructions. We inwardly groan whenever he arrives.

'That's it, dear, put your face near to it, just move your shoulder round to the right, yes, that's right, looking good – just keep smiling – can you just reach up slightly towards the table, that's lovely – now he's turning to face you, so we'll go for this one, keep smiling and looking at the camera and oh – that would have been a good one but he just moved a bit too quick – you couldn't just get him to do that again . . .' The commentary goes on and on and eventually even the animal starts to look fed up – let alone you. And which one do they print in the paper the next day? The one with both of you looking fed up!

Mind you, dedication comes into this as well. Francis Stothard takes many pictures for our local newspaper, but will be best remembered for squeezing his very tall frame into a squirrel aviary together with one of our students, Shelley, a very attractive young lady. She had rather stupidly told Francis that the squirrel would take a nut from her mouth and Francis was sure this would be the picture of the day.

With both of them crammed in the aviary complete with grey squirrels doing circuits around the wire with excitement, it was a pity that we did not have a camera on the outside. Shelley stood with pouting mouth complete with peanut, Francis endeavouring to be in the right position ready for action. The three squirrels were amazed at all this attention and did their usual trick of urinating as they chased around the cage. Despite all this Francis was still keen to get the shot, but I must admit that a careless remark from us outside about the danger of them crawling up his trouser leg unsettled him and, I'm afraid, he decided to call it a day! It was sweet justice for all the times he had asked *us* to do the impossible.

When I wrote my last book, Francis asked me if I would sign it for him. He could show it off to the office, he teased. My inscription read as follows:

To Francis, for all the positions you have got me in over the years, especially 52 and number 105, best wishes, Pauline.

I wonder if he did?

Derek would rarely get caught up in the photo calls, but he did one year when we were given a goose that had turned up near our local beach. We thought it was a white-fronted goose, but someone visiting thought that it was a lesser white-fronted goose, which is evidently very rare in Somerset, and before we knew it the 'twitchers' (as avid bird-watchers who specialize in rare sightings are nicknamed) started to arrive. There is evidently very little difference between the two species, and one probably has to be a lesser white-fronted goose to recognize another.

On hearing of our rare species, a photographer for a newspaper arrived unexpectedly and, in the absence of me and any of the girls, Derek was talked into having his photograph taken complete with goose under his arm. Having been interrupted whilst cleaning the cows out, Derek had his old clothes on and looked slightly dishevelled. When his mother saw the photograph in the paper the following morning, she remarked that it reminded her of his school photographs. Looking closely at this photograph of a grown man complete with beard and looking somewhat bemused, I failed to see what she meant. 'I mean,' said his mother, 'that I wish that I had been there beforehand with a comb!' We received a very serious letter, shortly after the article had been in the paper, from Sir Peter Scott, advising us that it was just an ordinary white-fronted goose – so our claim to fame did not last.

Dotty's photograph was something a little bit different. We had an advertising firm contact us for a photograph of a pig, to be part of an advertising campaign stating that pigs could fly. The idea was, using a computer, to superimpose wings on to a very clear black and white photograph of a pig.

We had, at the time, a very tame pig called Dotty and the representative from the firm called to see if Dotty was suitable. The photographer with him was concerned that she had to be as clean as possible for her debut. As he had already mentioned the fee of £50, Derek was keen to be involved. Leading her out of her pen, Dotty was taken into the yard and given a complete body workover with washing-up liquid and rubbed dry until she was as pink as a newborn piglet. All this was taken completely in her stride and, for once in our lives, it went off without a hitch. Dotty posed for the camera beautifully and within two hours the job was done. A very happy Derek had £50 in his pocket, probably the only time he became involved with publicity work quite so willingly! The photograph worked well and because of its unusual nature it was featured in several papers, just because of the novelty value. We must be the only people to have owned a flying pig.

We have been lucky enough to have had several articles in magazines, but one scoop was an article in one of the leading national newspapers, centre spread. The reporter had to come down from London by train and we offered to collect her from the station. She was a tall willowy young lady, who spent the

entire day with us, interviewing both Derek and myself. Her name was Jane and she was fascinated by the variety of animals to be seen here, especially the badger cubs that I was hand-rearing at the time.

While she was with me, we discussed the serious issues concerning badgers and their persecution. Her contact with us had been through the conservation officer of the National Federation of Badger Groups, as the article she was writing was to be on badger groups and the work they carry out. By sending Jane to us with the opportunity of seeing live badgers, the Federation was hoping that the badger groups would receive some publicity and gain some new members. We also talked about the variety of wild creatures that find their way here.

When she was with Derek, she asked how he had adapted to having the general public around all the time. Luckily Derek does not mind people around him, but he said that he doubted that his father would have liked the lifestyle as it was a far cry from the quiet days when just the local boys would come and work on the farm in return for a glass of cider.

Jane queried how we were able to finance our work and Derek explained about the Bluebell Sett Wildlife Appeal, a group of people who through membership or sponsoring an animal help us pay the inevitable bills. 'Some of our members come regularly to visit, such as those two ladies in the tearoom', said Derek and he pointed to a couple of ladies, Angela Lee and Eileen Mitchell. They were having a cream tea in our tearoom. We have come to know Eileen and Angela quite well through their frequent visits. They work as tour guides on the Continent and are extremely attractive ladies, very well dressed and highly articulate.

Derek introduced Jane to Eileen and Angela, explaining to them that Jane was a reporter who had been asking about the Bluebell Sett. Both of them enthused over our work and stressed how important they thought it all was. A chance remark from Eileen at the end of the conversation was: 'We love it here, we're just two dotty old ladies that come whenever we can, to see all the animals and support Derek and Pauline in the work that they do.'

By the end of the day, Jane's arm must have been aching from all the writing that she was constantly doing, as she made notes on everything she saw. Derek drove her back to the station to catch her train. 'Well,' he said, when he got back, 'it's going to be some article if all the writing she was doing is anything to go by!'

It certainly was! As the article was issued on the Saturday before Whitsun, we hoped that they might mention us as well as the badger groups, and encourage visitors our way. When I opened the paper, I could not believe my eyes. It was a double-page article with pictures of our animals. The part on the badger groups was a small piece about two columns wide and three inches down. The rest was on us – how a farmer's wife saved badgers and other wildlife despite her grumpy old husband who was complaining that he could not get any food because the kitchen was full of badger cubs. Described as 'all whiskers and west-country accent', he was quoted as saying he was fed up with all the mess and was happier with his pigs! He used to have a good social life when it was cider and dairy cows, but now it was all badgers and tourists and it's all the wife's fault.

Worse was to come. Derek was quoted as saying 'English people love badgers and lots are joining badger groups now, mostly dotty old ladies.' This, carried on the editorial, was directed at two tour guides, Angela Lee and Eileen Mitchell, who had called into the farm for tea.

I am sure that, to this day, there are some people in the badger groups who read this article and still won't talk to me. The main trouble is that because it's in the paper, readers think that it's true. (I must admit – we did get some people visit, just to see the grumpy old man and his poor suffering wife.) Derek, quite understandably, was livid. We also felt very embarrassed for Eileen and Angela. Luckily they had a good laugh about it, but not everyone has that kind of sense of humour.

With all the different animals that come to us, we spend a lot of time at the vet's! We tend to have one main vet, who as much as possible will attend our animals and get to know our establishment, although obviously, because it is a busy practice, there are several vets employed there.

Up until recently, Barry Parsons did most of our work. A very quiet person, he had a wonderful way with anything that we took into him, no matter how large or small it was. From a roaring badger to a minuscule baby dormouse, he would gently examine it, soothing the animal as he worked, and was prepared to go to great lengths to try and get them better. It was with great regret that we heard he was leaving the practice, and changing course in his career in order to spend more time with his young family. Over a period of time, you build up a relationship of trust with someone with whom you share the joys and sorrows of caring for animals, and it was difficult to get used to the fact that Barry would no longer be there. With all the qualities that he has to offer, I sincerely hope he will return to the profession again, once his family has grown up. We would love to see him back.

His replacement could not have been more different as far as personality was concerned, but the care and attention was still the same. Stuart Murray was from New Zealand. Tall (dark and handsome!), he was very assertive in his manner with a wicked sense of humour. He had a wonderful drawl and a very laid-back attitude, but he too, as Barry had, would take time to explain the reason for the illness and why it presented such symptoms, and help you understand what is going on inside the part of the body that is having problems. Little did I know that, later, Stuart was going to help me through one of the most difficult times of my life.

I went into the vet's to have a badger X-rayed and Stuart took me into the back to show me the results. Whilst discussing it with him, I felt a little cold nose nudging my leg and looked down to see who had joined us. A little black and brown 'thing' wriggled its floppy body in greeting, with its bald tail wagging, pleased that someone was talking to it. It was meant to be a black and tan puppy but most of the hair was missing from the tail and rear end and the whole of its body and face was covered in scabs. Even so, with folded ears pressed flat to the sides of his head with excitement, the soft brown eyes pleaded for a fuss.

'You're a mangy old thing,' I murmured, fondling his head.

He was quickly followed by a young girl, with her long hair tied back in a pony tail.

'Got it in one,' said Becky, the veterinary nurse, who had been guilty of letting him out of his cage for a bit of exercise and was looking for him. 'He came from the RSPCA and he's had sarcoptic mange. He's on the mend but he looks so awful nobody wants him and,' she said, looking straight at me, 'he's going in the bin bag on Monday if we can't find anyone to give him a home.'

I tried to keep my attention on what Stuart was saying about the X-ray, but the little body weaving in and out of my legs made sure that Becky's words stayed in my mind. Once our discussion was over, I picked the puppy up and was rewarded with licks all over my face until I was able to restrain him. He was only the size of a Jack Russell but with longer legs. Trying to be sensible, I put him down. Back out at reception, Becky collared me again.

'Sweet, isn't he?' she remarked.

'Well, you certainly can't call him pretty,' I remarked. 'Where did he come from?'

'He was stolen from a traveller and taken to the RSPCA. Evidently the mother and the four pups all had mange, but he was the worst and could hardly stand when he came in, but he seems to be picking up, although he has got a diet problem as well,' she explained. Laughing, she said to me: 'Tempted?'

'I'll go and work on Derek, but don't hold your breath!' I replied with a smile.

Becky has been a veterinary nurse at the surgery for several years now and has quite a few dogs herself. It was she who talked me into having a puppy only a year before. Polly was a tiny mite and a very sickly puppy. I eventually decided there was something wrong with her, and when she was checked by the vet and given an X-ray, it was found that she had a shunt between her liver and her heart. This was an extra vein that stopped the blood from being cleaned properly, and because of its position it was inoperable. This gave her a life expectancy of only six months. Polly made seven months, but her short little life brought me a lot of joy and, as with all pets, we have our memories.

I had never replaced Polly as we still had our two sons' dogs to look after now they were away at university: Barney, who is a mongrel but looks more like a teddy bear, and Samantha, a neurotic miniature schnauzer, who barks when people come in, while they are there and when they go!

My mind was working on how to broach the subject with Derek as I drove home. I just couldn't forget those brown eyes. We were going out for a meal that evening with some friends and I waited for the drive home to just 'mention' the puppy. It had been a very enjoyable evening; Derek had had a few drinks and I just passed the time as I drove home, saying what a shame it was that the puppy was going to be put down. Derek was probably way ahead of me as he, by now, knows me through and through. But there was not too much of an objection put forward, and I thought I was in with a chance.

I bided my time the next morning, until coffee break, and then asked if Derek would mind my having the puppy. He did, but knowing there would be no peace, and on my head be it, I could go and fetch it. 'As long' was the proviso 'as it has no Alsatian in it.'

Excited, I grabbed the car keys, told Mandy I could have the puppy (because she was in on it as well!) and went to get him. 'I can have him,' I said to Becky, as soon as I arrived at the surgery, 'as long as he has no Alsatian in him.'

'Right,' said Becky. 'In that case – he's a collie cross.'

Stuart, who had been behind the desk, raised his eyebrows. Smiling he said, 'You know we don't know how old he really is, and you could have problems again, are you sure you want to take him on?' But looking at the pair of us, he knew he was wasting his breath. Becky went and got him for me. Placing him in the front of the car with a bag of special diet dog food that was nearly three times as big as he was, he curled up in his blanket and slept all the way to his new home. We were soon back at the farm. 'Well,' I said to him, as I took him out of the car, 'I've got to call you something.' And remembering Stuart's bemused face, I decided to call him Murray, the same as Stuart's surname.

Carrying Murray in through the yard to the front garden, I set him down on the front lawn, by which time most of the staff had come to look at the new arrival. Surprisingly, no one was impressed with this pot-bellied, bandy-legged, bald and scabby puppy, but it wasn't very long before the little body was weaving through the numerous legs and winning them over in the same way as he had with me – except maybe Derek. I hadn't actually realized how badly Murray walked; on examining him, his hocks were very thick and hard as if he had walked on them for some time when, maybe, he had not the strength in his legs to stand on his feet. When he sat, the elbows of his front legs turned out, giving the appearance of a very camp little dog!

'He looks the same colour as an Alsatian to me,' remarked Derek.

'Well, yes,' I replied slowly, choosing my words carefully, 'but then lots of dogs are black and tan, even Yorkshire terriers. With his ears folded over like that he could even be a long-legged dachshund.'

Derek was not convinced.

Murray was a super puppy apart from the usual puddles and poops; he was very quiet and was no trouble at night. The only problem we had with him was visitors feeding him. To begin with, I did not let him out of my sight because he looked so awful; we needed to explain why we had this mangy-looking thing, but slowly the hair started to come back. He soon started to explore his new surroundings, and on his little forays, Samantha started to teach him how to find visitors eating picnics!

He only had to eat a tiny morsel of anything other than his diet biscuit and his motions became very loose. Things came to a head one evening when I had left Derek in charge of him while I was outside talking to a friend. Murray so far had been unable to win Derek over as an admirer and the fact that Murray's ears were beginning to stand up with a slight similarity to an Alsatian was not really helping the situation. Unbeknown to me, Murray had obviously been fed something that upset him and whilst Derek will tackle anything from calving cows to mucking out, he is unable to deal with vomit and dog's mess.

Returning to the kitchen an hour or so later, I found Derek in the armchair with his feet up watching the football.

'Your dog,' accused Derek, 'has not been content with making the most awful smells in this room, but has been heaving and vomiting for the past half hour and I'm not prepared to move from this chair as there cannot be much of the floor left to safely walk on!'

A very dejected-looking Murray sat in the opposite corner, his ears sliding down the side of his head, shoulders hunched and drooling at the mouth. A more sorrowful sight you could not expect to see. Once the all-clear was sounded for Derek to be able to move freely in his own home once more, I set to with cardboard and felt pens and made a large disc out of yellow card with a message on each side – DO NOT FEED COS I GET SICK. With this hung from his collar, his forays may still have included finding visitors with picnics, but he came away empty-handed (or should it be empty-stomached?).

Soon Murray's coat was a sleek black and tan with no sign of the nasty scabs, and he grew and he grew and he grew. Temperament-wise, he is as soft as they come; and when his bark became a deep throaty sound, Murray would sit in the yard and bark and then look round to see where the sound came from!

When he went back to the vet's for his inoculation, the nurses were amazed at how he had grown. Taking him in to see Stuart, I placed Murray on to the table. Stuart got the inoculation card out for his records.

'Name?' Stuart queried.

'Murray,' I said with a smile.

'Yes, I had heard he had been named after me', he said. 'Still,'

said Stuart, turning his attention to Murray, 'you're quite a smart dog now, living up to the name, heh?'

Writing on the card, Stuart came to the section to be filled in naming the breed. 'German Shepherd X' – he entered, then in brackets, he wrote: 'If Derek is reading this – Yorkshire Terrier X Collie'!

By the time the lambing season started early in the spring, Murray was still only seven months old – a real teenager! Now slightly resembling a horse, he was still teething and the table and chairs teetered on legs that were chewed nearly all the way through. But he was still very gentle and wouldn't say boo to a goose. Murray was fascinated when the first of the pet lambs came to the kitchen for the first few days of their lives. Charlie was a Jacob lamb. Black and white and very pretty, there was nothing really wrong with him other than his mother had given birth to triplets and did not have enough milk for all of them. While Charlie was in for his bottle, Murray would play with him and they became firm friends.

Yet again the newspaper rang looking for an animal story. I said that we were still very quiet and had nothing to interest them, but mentioned the friendship between Charlie and Murray which they could use if they were really desperate.

Within minutes Francis, the photographer, rang to say yes, they would like to come and take the picture. As usual, Francis wanted the impossible and we even put chocolate spread on the lamb's head to get Murray to lick it. Francis still wanted to try other shots. After a lot of time and effort, we managed to get a shot of Murray holding the baby's bottle with the lamb sucking it at the same time. Pleased with the results, the photographer went away, assuring me that we would be mentioned in the article.

Splashed across the pages the next day was a lovely picture of Murray with Charlie and a completely fictitious heading: DAN-GEROUS DOG TURNS DEVOTED DAD TO BABY LAMB. This was followed by an equally fictitious story of how this dangerous dog, secretly rescued by Pauline Kidner from a lethal injection due to his aggressive nature, had turned into a big softie at heart and was now helping rear an orphaned lamb.

It may not be in the same league, but Charles and Di – you have my every sympathy!

However, it must be admitted that I have been known to lie myself (although not very often!). March to April brings us our intake of fox cubs, and one paper came and did the story of a fox cub that we had which was only a matter of a few weeks old. If we can get any publicity on fox cubs, it is always useful because it can mean we have the chance to ask people not to pick them up unless they are absolutely sure they are orphaned. In so many cases, the general public pick cubs up thinking they are orphaned just because they cannot see an adult, but usually, especially if they are out playing, they are just enjoying the sunshine and will return to their earth when they are tired. Others pick them up having mistaken them for puppies, not realizing that fox cubs are chocolate brown when first born. Foxes are very difficult to find release sites for once old enough to go, so to pick up fox cubs that may not need help is merely putting increased pressure on an already existing problem.

In fact the paper did a nice article on it, and it was worth doing. We rarely keep fox cubs for very long, as the last thing you want is for them to become tame, so once they are weaned we pass them on to the RSPCA Wildlife Unit near Taunton. There they are put in very large enclosures to help them remain wild, ready for their eventual release back into the wild.

A month or so later the same paper rang back, asking if they could do a follow-on story to the one already done on the cub, seeing how he was doing and how much he had grown. Well of course, the original cub had already passed on to the RSPCA, but we had one in that was the same size as it would have been by now. This one had been hand-reared by veterinary nurses from a nearby town. Unfortunately, she was too tame for release so she had been put with our domesticated foxes. 'Yes, that's fine,' I said, thinking 'well, they won't know one cub from another', but for the life of me, I could not remember the name of the original cub that the story was about. So, when the photographer was here, I made sure that I did not mention her name and neither did the photographer. I had nearly got away with it when, without thinking, as I put her back, I said, 'There you go Hazel, back with the others.'

'Hazel!' said the photographer, 'I was trying to think what her name was and couldn't remember.'

'Oh,' I said weakly, thinking, 'well if he can't remember, perhaps it won't matter.'

'The reporter will ring you for the details', said the photographer, packing away all his gear. 'Thanks again, Pauline.'

When the reporter rang through, we chatted over the details.

'Hazel was the name, wasn't it?' came the question.

'Well,' I hedged, 'yes, that's right.' I crossed my fingers.

'That's a funny name for a boy,' said the reporter, 'because it was a male cub, wasn't it, that we photographed before?'

'Yes, that's right', I replied, thinking quickly. 'Well, you know how it is, people bring things in having already given them a name, and they don't always check to see what they are first! The name just sort of stuck.' I laughed.

So did she – I'd got away with it.

Feeling guilty at my lies, I was made to feel even worse the next day, when the local television picked the story up from the paper and came to film the fox 'with the identity crisis'.

Oh, what an evil web we weave, when first we practise to deceive! I shall never go to heaven, but then there will be a lot of reporters to keep me company!

Especially through the winter, I travel and give talks about the work of the Bluebell Sett and the venues and audiences vary tremendously. One of the first talks I gave was to a group at Clevedon. It was mainly retired people who were going to be there. Still slightly new to it all, I was a little nervous, and on pulling in at the venue, I noticed there were only three or four cars. Hardly anybody there, I thought, we shall just be able to sit in a circle and I can chat about the slides. On opening the door, to my horror, I saw nearly a hundred people waiting and I was to be up on a stage with a microphone. Once I get started, probably because I love the subject so much, I find it easy to talk. At the end, two elderly ladies came up and complimented me on my talk. 'It was lovely,' said one, 'I heard every word.'

'Yes,' said the other. 'Really interesting. In fact, I don't think anybody fell asleep this afternoon!'

Compliment indeed.

At another talk, near Weston-super-Mare, when I had finished, a kindly gent was helping me out with all my equipment. As I had gone through the door I had dropped a slide from my case. Standing holding my table under one arm, the gentleman called to me that I had dropped a slide. With one leg wedging the door open, and the other steadying the table, he stood with the slide underneath him. Bending over to pick the slide up, I thanked him for pointing it out to me. With eyes twinkling he smiled and said jokingly, 'It's a long time since I've had a lady your age between my legs.' I giggled – it wasn't the kind of remark I was expecting!

One talk I shall never forget is one that we organized with Simon King. Simon is well known for his wildlife filming and dramas that he does with the BBC. He lives locally and was kind enough to be our founder Patron of the Bluebell Sett Wildlife Appeal which we started in order to finance our work. Early in 1994 he offered to do a talk for us about all his film work and how he gets different effects. The money raised was to help us finance our centre. To start with we hoped to hire a tent and organize the evening at the centre, but perhaps that idea was a bit too ambitious so early in the year. About a month before the event was meant to take place, we decided that, because the land was so waterlogged, to hold the event in a tent was practically impossible so we looked for an alternative venue. Our difficulty was in finding a room that would hold 200 people.

Eventually Derek had a brainwave, and suggested a local holiday camp. He had met the manager on several occasions and so he rang and explained the situation. Luckily there was a room on the camp site that would hold 200 people, and it was available for the night that we required, so we booked it. Some tickets to the event had already been sold, so we asked the manager to send us a map of how to get to the camp site so that we could forward this on to the ticketholders, explaining that the venue had been changed. The map duly arrived and we photocopied it, and sent a copy to everyone attending the event.

The day drew near and we organized video equipment and amplification all to arrive about three hours prior to the performance. We kept in touch with Simon, explaining that the venue had been changed and arranging final schedules for the event.

Our first big mistake was not to have checked out the venue beforehand. I arrived at the holiday camp in the early afternoon ready to meet the technicians and put the finishing touches to the seating plan. We had managed to sell 180 tickets, and hoped that with the publicity in local papers we would pick up a few chance arrivals. I made my way to reception as soon as I arrived at the camp and the receptionist explained to me where the room for the talk was. Following the instructions, I soon began to realize that not everyone was going to find it very easily – down the road, turn right, past the slot machine area, through the ballroom, past the bar . . .

As I neared the ballroom I met the technician, who was also trying to get into the room. It was all locked up and no one seemed to know who had the keys. One of the receptionists went in search of the foreman and we both waited. Standing waiting by the entrance, I started to read the notices inside the ballroom door and began to worry as I saw a casino night and disco advertised for that very evening in the ballroom. I prayed that we were going to be quite a distance from there.

Eventually the keys were found and we were taken through to our booked venue. I immediately noticed that the ballroom was right next to where we were going to be. Opening the doors into our room the technician noticed that they had not allowed the 20 feet that he required for the rear projection. There was, in fact, no way that the screen and seating for 200 could fit into this room.

Walking down to the other end of the room, I looked through the door at the end to find that it opened into the kitchens of the dining-room. Tables of stainless steel gleamed, dishwashers and kitchen utensils lined the walls. Great! A disco at one end of a room that would not hold enough people, and a kitchen at the other end with the clatter of china and cutlery being washed up.

It is at times like these that it would be nice to have someone else to blame, but it was completely our own fault.

The manager arrived and I began to voice my fears. Luckily the kitchen was not going to be used that evening, but I still had my doubts as to whether the disco would keep the music turned down. The technician got the equipment in as tight as he could, but we still only had seating for 170. We just had to hope that there would not be more. I made my way out to the car to find the last few things to go in and as I did, Linda Groves, one of our committee members from the Bluebell Sett, arrived in her car.

'What a mess!' she exclaimed as she got out of the car.

'Yes, I know,' I said, without realizing we were talking about different things.

'You've heard then?' she queried.

'No,' I said, becoming aware that Linda was not talking about any of the problems that I had discovered.

'You know the map that we sent out to everyone?' she asked. Slowly I nodded.

'Well, it's the wrong map. The directions will take everyone to the other holiday camp of this group at Berrow,' she wailed.

Berrow is about three miles from where we were standing.

Frantically trying to make some sense out of this ghastly situation, I explained about how difficult it was to find the room in the first place, and now with everyone going to the wrong holiday camp, it was going to be a nightmare. We made some plans: I would go back to the farm and change. Derek arranged to go to the other holiday camp and would direct everyone back to here. In the meantime, I would quickly do some signs to help everyone find the room once they arrived at the right camp. Linda was left to hold the fort and wait for Simon King to arrive, while I tried to sort things out.

It was one time in my life when, if there had been a hole in the ground, I would have willingly jumped in and disappeared. With Derek on his way to redirect everyone, I got back to the camp and placed strategic notices with arrows showing the audience, if they ever arrived, where we were.

Simon had arrived ahead of me and I found both he and Linda in fits of laughter. The whole thing had deteriorated to such an extent that they could do nothing else but laugh. During his talk, Simon had explained to Linda, he would be showing several excerpts from his films to demonstrate the techniques of film-making.

Consequently he would require the light to be turned on and off about every ten minutes or so. Simon had decided to run through it with Linda so that she would understand what he meant, but when it had come to it, they had both been unable to find any light switches. Eventually they had had to get the manager down, who then explained that the lights were controlled in the adjacent fish and chip shop. So every time the lights had to be switched on or off, Linda had to go into the kitchens at the back of the room, bang on the tiled wall and shout 'OK, Margaret' to the lady serving in the chip shop, who would duly turn them off or on.

Any lesser man than Simon would have walked out on us and left us to sort the mess out ourselves, but he was fantastic. He greeted everyone as they arrived, apologizing for any inconvenience caused by the error in the directions. Luckily we managed to squeeze everyone in. The disco did keep the music turned down, and Simon enthralled them all with his talk; he even managed to make the whole thing of 'banging on the wall for Margaret in the chip shop to turn the lights off' into such an amusing event that I'm sure some of them must have thought it was part of the act. He even suggested that at the end of the evening, to show their appreciation to Margaret, they could all pop in for a bag of chips – and he proceeded to go round himself too!

Simon has helped us in many ways, and he has always been charming and approachable in every way. Maybe there is no risk of him rising to any heady heights of grandeur whilst his young children answer the phone. When I telephoned through to Simon one day, his young son answered.

'Hallo,' I said, 'is Daddy there?'

'Wait a minute and I'll go and get him,' the little voice replied.

I heard him run up the stairs and a mumbled conversation followed. Coming back to the phone, Simon's son proudly announced, very matter of factly, 'Daddy's on the toilet at the moment, but he's just wiping his bottom and then he will be down.' The telephone receiver went down on the table and he skipped away.

A few minutes later, Simon arrived and picked up the phone.

'I,' I teased, 'know what you've been doing.'

'I know,' Simon groaned, 'I heard, I just hoped it was someone that I knew!'

We have at different times been involved with television. One programme that we featured in was 'Talk to the Animals', a very popular show that they broadcast in Australia. We enjoyed the filming of that one because the crew were so laid-back and really had a laugh over different things. But this was one time that, afterwards, we said, 'well that won't bring any visitors in, being shown in Australia'; however, so far we have already had seven parties from Australia who have included us in their English tour because we were featured on the programme – so you never know.

Some things are contrived and others just happen naturally. When the BBC came to do a short news item on the opening of our badger observation sett, they were taking a shot of the three badgers that I had hand-reared, out playing in the interpretation side of the sett. The badgers were still only juveniles, full of fun, and were busy exploring the seating and displays. Much to the amusement of the film crew, Primrose stood on her hind legs and pulled down a booklet called *The Problems with Badgers*. Tearing the front cover off, she proceeded to shuffle backwards towards their bedding chambers, dragging this offensive cover with her, as if to say that if she had anything to do with it, this was one book that was not going to be on show!

Not all the presenters are happy with the directives they are given. West Country Television arranged for one of their presenters to come and do a short piece on the decline of the barn owl, with our tame barn owl on his shoulder, without finding out first if he even liked owls. It turned out that he was absolutely terrified of them, and I have never seen anyone look as uncomfortable as he did throughout the whole of the interview, trying to keep his head as far away as possible from his own shoulder, which of course is physically impossible!

Another one from West Country Television was sent to film the six badger cubs that we had living in the kitchen. The presenter and cameraman had decided that, as all the cubs were sound asleep behind the chair, the easiest thing to do was slowly move the chair away and for the presenter to do his piece to camera, with the cubs in the background before they woke up. This did in fact look as if it was going to work, as the cubs all stayed sound asleep, but the presenter kept fluffing his lines. One of the cubs woke up and meandered off, and the cameraman began to realize that time was running out before they would all be on the move. Talking it through in his head the presenter nodded: 'OK,' he said, 'I've got it now.' Crouching down for the seventh time, the presenter watched the cameraman. 'And roll', said the cameraman, motioning that he had started to film. The presenter went into his spiel. Word perfect, it was going fine. Standing behind the cameraman, I watched as the cub that had moved off came back and joined the others in the background of the presenter, who was drawing to the end of his piece – it had gone without a hitch. Yawning, the returning cub nuzzled the other sleeping cubs and quite clearly, on camera, started to comfort-suck the penis of another male cub.

The presenter finished his piece, waited a minute and then exclaimed, 'Yes! That's the one we'll use, it went perfectly.' The cameraman hung his head. 'Er, no,' he said, 'I don't think so!'

When 'Country Watch' came, Susan King had to conduct an interview with me exercising some bats in our kitchen. Standing waiting for the instruction to start, she was steeling herself to be all right when I took them out of their container. Even so, as they climbed out and started to fly, she let out an uncontrollable, strangled scream. The film crew just fell about laughing, and were so amused that they kept that part in!

The more you become involved with wildlife films, the more you understand how certain shots are achieved, and gain an insight into the incredible dedication and time that goes into programmes that we accept as the norm these days. In a way, it is a little bit like the newspapers: we believe everything we see and hear, without questioning that bits and pieces cut from a film can alter the whole emphasis of what is seen. Many of Simon King's drama films are so cleverly filmed that he is often accused of causing cruelty to the animals concerned in order to obtain a certain shot, when in fact nothing could be further from the truth.

Simon helped us with the dressing of our observation sett when it was created in 1989, in the hope that when he came to do his film 'Dusk the Badger' there was a possibility that we might have cubs in there that he could film. He made his badger film in 1991 and Bluebell waited until 1992 to have her cubs. So it just shows you that two years prior to making a film, he was already making plans for it – some would work, others didn't.

In the film 'Dusk the Badger', there is a sequence where a dog is seen going down into a badger sett where it fights with the badger underground. All this was made possible by the use of puppets. A lady with a tame badger got it used to playing with a dog puppet, and a dog with a badger puppet. With clever cutting of film and overlaying, it gave a very lifelike action of a real fight.

After the showing of the film, I had a very irate lady on the phone accusing Simon of dreadful cruelty in order to gain these effects. I tried to explain that it was all done with puppets and no animal was stressed or hurt in any way. 'Oh, it was real all right,' she exclaimed, 'I could hear from the sounds that the dog and the badger were making.' I then explained that the sounds are all created after the film is made, because very rarely does the chance to film and sound-record come at the same time, especially in the wild.

As an example, I told her about the Vietnamese pig, Rosie, that we used to have. If there was one thing Rosie would do, it was squeal. If you had to move her from one house to another, she made a terrible noise. Simon came and did a sound recording as we were moving her one day, but not because he wanted the sound of a pig: he used it as a sound effect for a wildebeest being killed by a lion. Not only what you see, but also what you hear, cannot always be believed!

Most recently, Simon has filmed for 'Tyto the Barn Owl' and a special aviary was built here for part of the filming. A captive-bred pair of barn owls were kept in the aviary so that Simon could film the breeding of these birds without disturbing the barn owls rearing young that he was filming in the wild. A chimney and roof were

the fight . . . was all done with puppets . . .

built in the aviary to match the house in the wild that Simon was filming. Even the same tile was missing from the roof, so that parts of the film taken in the wild could be cut to match parts of film taken here. I can remember Simon and Allan, who helped him with his filming, arriving here about 10 p.m. one evening and staying until 5.30 the following morning. Later that day, Simon was telling us how pleased he was with the filming he had done through the night. 'I should think', he said enthusiastically, 'that I've got at least a minute and a half to two minutes of television from it.' As I have said before, we really do under-estimate the time and effort that goes into a programme that we sit down and watch for half an hour or so, without comprehending that at times it has taken a year, maybe more, to produce it.

One of our real highlights has to be when we were asked to be filmed for the programme 'Animal Country' with Desmond Morris and Sarah Kennedy. This is a series that goes out in the winter at a popular time of 6 p.m. on a Sunday. Desmond Morris and Sarah Kennedy are seen driving around in a Land Rover, going to many different places where people work with all kinds of animals. It is also a competition, so that at the end of the series, whoever they feel has done the most for animals within the series is presented with a cut-glass plate and an award of £3,000.

They came to us in August, and luckily one of the leverets that we had hand-reared was old enough then to be released and we were able to film actually letting it go, back into the field where it had been found several months beforehand. Both Sarah Kennedy and Desmond Morris were very easy to talk to and had a way of making you feel relaxed. It was a pleasure to meet both of them and we were very lucky that, when we approached him, Desmond Morris agreed to be a patron of the Bluebell Sett as well.

The crew had to return to take different shots of the animals that we have here and, again, they were a crew that was a pleasure to have around. I was tricked into thinking that they had some extra air-time, and was asked if they could come back and do a small piece talking about the badgers and Dot, the deer; and of course, I agreed. Nobody could have been more surprised than me when, with cameras rolling, Sarah Kennedy explained to me that there was no extra air-time and they were really here to present the cheque and the glass plate – we were the winners of the series. It was a wonderful feeling: £3,000 to put towards the enclosures that we so desperately needed and, of course, the honour of winning such a prize. With so many worthwhile causes shown on the series, I feel very humble to have been chosen for the award. I just wish we could all have been winners.

5

Tortoises and Turtles

I had not realized, until we took some to an agricultural show, that most children these days have never seen a tortoise. We had to fill a large tent with animals for visitors to see and decided to build a pen of straw bales and allow the children to go in with the tortoises and feed them. We took tortoises of all ages and sizes and people were fascinated. No one was allowed to pick them up, but we gave the children lettuce and greens to feed the tortoises with.

I noticed one lad who was trying to feed a tortoise with a dandelion leaf. A lady had drawn me into conversation and I was unable to break off from talking to her, to give the small boy some advice. No matter how much he tried, he just could not get the tortoise to take any notice of the food that he was offering it.

Eventually the lady moved away, and I called to the little lad.

'Having trouble getting the tortoise to eat the food?' I queried.

'Yes,' he said, 'I don't think he wants it.'

'Maybe, if you tried to feed the other end, you might get some response,' I advised him, smiling. He had just spent the past ten minutes offering the food to the tail end of the tortoise. When the boy rectified his mistake, the tortoise tucked into the offered food with gusto!

I myself can remember having tortoises as pets when I was a child and many people remark about how cheap they were in the 'old days'. They certainly were not respected as pets in those days, and owners would think nothing of drilling holes into their shells to attach a piece of string to them so they could not disappear. Even if they did disappear or die during hibernation in the winter, it was no problem because you just went out the next year and bought another one!

They are incredible creatures and are one of the oldest reptiles to have survived from the time when the first animals began to live on this earth. Tortoises have been with us since prehistoric times, changing little in their appearance except that the thick scaly plates that covered the body have now become a shell. Basically, the tortoise has its skeleton on the outside.

Tortoises and their close relations, turtles, have had a very varied history, from being considered a sacred animal by the Egyptians, to having their shells used for musical instruments or ornaments. Turtles are also considered a gastronomic delight or

even an aphrodisiac. It was in the 1890s that they became popular as pets. Easy to catch due to their slowness, at the beginning of the twentieth-century between 100,000 and 150,000 were being imported into Britain from the Mediterranean every year. Stacked in crates, with no thoughts for their welfare, a very high percentage did not survive the journey; and of the few that did, most died within their first year before they were able to adapt to the British climate.

From 1890 to 1984, it was estimated that the numbers imported into Britain exceeded 10 million. Considering that, in the right conditions, a tortoise can live for up to 100 years, I don't think many could have survived, otherwise we would be overrun with them! Happily, legislation was brought in to ban all imports of Mediterranean tortoises, and now the only way to obtain one is to acquire one of the survivors from the importation days or to purchase a tortoise that has been hatched here. The price of a tortoise now can vary from £50 to £250 and, when you consider how few there are around, they must be worth that kind of money. High prices hopefully mean that people acquiring them will take the trouble to find out how to look after them properly.

When we started our open farm, we were offered our first tortoise by a local person and the numbers slowly increased. Ask someone what a tortoise eats, and they will usually immediately tell you that their diet consists of lettuce, tomato and cucumber; but they will eat a far more diverse selection of food than that, from vegetables and fruit even to cornflakes!

The group name for tortoises, turtles and terrapins is chelonians, so if any of you are wanting information on how to keep any of these creatures, join the Chelonian Group where they will tell you all you need to know. You even get this incredible book that tells you just about everything from housing, feeding and breeding, right down to the little-known facts such as – goose dung is poisonous to tortoises! I bet you didn't know that.

It was a book that one of the television producers should have read! I don't know if you can remember but a few years back a commercial was running on television showing a certain breed of tortoise, which was a Box tortoise. The advert proclaimed that this tortoise would show no interest if offered a lettuce from a normal fridge, but if it was placed next to a lettuce just taken out of a special crisper box in a new kind of fridge, the tortoise practically charged towards the lettuce, so keen was he to eat it.

Had the producer done his homework he would have found out that a Box tortoise lives on insects and would never eat lettuce, even if it was pushed into his mouth!

We were advertising some ducklings that we had reared on the farm and a delightful couple from Exmoor called in to purchase some. Their names were Peggy and Jack Leach. They themselves had been farmers and were now retired, but Jack still liked to keep a few chickens and ducks around.

Jack was short, with a weathered look, but his suntanned face had lines from a smiling disposition. He was in his shirt sleeves as it was a nice sunny day, with braces on his trousers. His hands showed a lifestyle of hard work and manual labour. Peggy was slim, and had a country way about her, with a bubbly personality that would see her through the ups and downs of farming life. We came to like both of them as friends very much. They chatted to us, fascinated by the centre, and Peggy told us of her tortoises that she had running free in her garden, all with different names. I took them round to see our tortoises.

Peggy confided in me that two of her females, Jemima and Gertie, usually lay eggs and that in the past they have hatched out. Keen to help us attract visitors, she asked me if I would like some eggs to try and hatch out. I was really keen. In the past we have done a lot of incubation with poultry, but to try and hatch out tortoises would be fascinating.

Incubation of eggs is a miracle in itself when you think about it, because an egg has to contain everything within it to produce a chick, tortoise or whatever. In a chicken's egg first the fertilized disc is placed within a shell, together with the white (called the albumen) and a yolk as the egg is laid. It will remain dormant unless constant heat of 37.5 degrees centigrade is applied, usually by a hen which has gone broody; the heat of her breast as she sits on them will warm the eggs under her to this temperature. It can also be done with an incubator. A hen will turn her eggs every 20 minutes from one side to the other. This is done because the fertilized disc attaches to the yolk as the egg starts to warm up and the embryo starts to grow, and by turning the egg, the hen stops the yolk from sticking to the side of the egg.

The creation of skin, blood, feathers and muscle is achieved mainly from the white fluid of the egg. Only 10 per cent of the yolk is used in the growing process. Calcium for the bones, beak and claws is taken from the shell, and as the time of hatching draws near, the shell becomes quite thin and feels like china as this chemical is absorbed from it.

The chick all this time has been living in the fluid of the egg. Unlike a mammal, joined by a placenta to its mother who continually eats throughout her pregnancy to supply the needs of the developing baby, everything that is required for the chick to form has to be contained in the egg as a separate unit.

As the chick develops, it is rolled in a ball with its head tucked under one wing. There is a space at the blunt end of the egg called an air sac. Just prior to hatching, nerves in the neck of the chick start to twitch causing the chick to push its head further under the wing. By now it will have a very small white dot on the tip of its beak, called an egg tooth; using this to penetrate the thin skin that lines the inside of the egg, through to the air sac, the chick takes its first breath.

The twitching in the neck becomes more severe and the constant moving action of the head under the wing eventually causes the egg tooth to pierce the shell of the egg, making the first hole. Then using the muscles in its shoulders, the chick rotates fractionally and starts to chip another hole next to the first one. Slowly and laboriously, the chick will rotate 360 degrees chipping holes as it goes, until the top of the egg drops off and the exhausted chick can climb out of the egg looking very wet and bedraggled. It will be a further 24 hours before it starts to look like the lovely fluffy chicks that we see in picture books.

While the chick is hatching, it absorbs the remainder of the egg yolk into its stomach to act as sustenance until the mother starts to feed it, or in the case of poultry and wading birds, until they are able to start looking for food themselves. The yolks in the eggs of birds whose chicks are self-supporting on hatching are much larger than the yolks in eggs of birds that are fed by their parents. This gives them extra food so that they can live for nearly 48 hours while they start to learn what is food and how and where to get it. This is why day-old chicks can be transported with no ill effects for the first day or so before being given a supply of fresh food and water. The egg tooth on the tip of the beak disappears at this time, after the first 24 hours.

I had seen many kinds of birds such as chicken, quail, peacocks and guinea-fowl hatch out, but the thought of hatching tortoises sounded very interesting. Peggy said she would let me know as soon as the tortoises laid the eggs and then we could go and pick them up. 'Usually between June and July, once it gets really warm, Gertie and Jemima start to dig holes all over the garden,' Peggy explained. 'This shows that they are thinking of laying their eggs and then it is up to me to watch them carefully!' She patted my arm. 'You wait,' she said, 'it won't be long.'

Waving goodbye to them as they left to go home, complete with the ducklings that they had purchased, I looked forward to hearing from them soon.

When Peggy rang to say that she had some eggs for me, she explained what Jemima and Gertie actually do. Once they had decided to lay their eggs, they backed up to the place they had chosen and slowly, with their back legs, they dug out a hole in the soil. Carefully moving slightly into the hole the tortoises then started to lay the eggs, which could be as many as seven or eight. When they had finished laying, they slowly and carefully covered the eggs over, gently stamping the soil down once they had finished. Indeed, if you were not watching, it would be difficult to find where the eggs had been laid. This is as much as the mother would do as normally, in the warmer climates, the temperature of the soil would start the incubation process. In Britain, the temperatures do not stay high enough for the 9- to 11-week period that tortoises require.

Although requiring a much longer incubation period than eggs laid by birds, they do not need as high a temperature: 70 to 80 degrees Fahrenheit is enough for them. What is most crucial is that they must not be tilted in any way. If the eggs are moved, they must be handled very carefully and kept in the same position as they were laid.

Peggy explained all this to me so that I would understand how to look after them, and also appreciate the importance of carrying them back to the farm without disturbing them. Derek and I thought we would use this as an excuse to go down together and collect the eggs. It is a lovely area where they live and we would enjoy the ride. 'Lovely,' said Peggy. 'We'll have some supper together.'

The drive down to where Peggy and Jack lived, just past Minehead, is not that easy as it is a road on which, once you get stuck behind a slow-moving vehicle, there is no way you can get past it for miles! On this occasion, the road was quiet and we could enjoy the glimpses of the sea as we drove through the hills and the rolling countryside, much of it covered in woodland, bracken or heather. Summer was at its height, with country flowers colouring the roadside verges. Herds of cows grazed lazily, swishing their tails at the unwanted flies that buzzed around them. We saw a pair of buzzards circling high above us, losing them from view and then glimpsing them again as we turned the corners of the winding road.

Soon we realized that we needed to keep our eyes on the road as we were nearing Peggy's house. As we turned away from the main road, a beautifully clear stream ran gurgling along the side of the road and we passed a very old brick bridge as we climbed up a steep and narrow lane. Suddenly we came upon the two cottages we were looking for. We parked the car by the hedge and opened the wooden gate into a lovely cottage garden. Old-fashioned flowers waved their heads in the warm breeze, bright pink mallows stood high by the stone wall leading to the front door, and deep blue delphiniums were a burst of colour against the collection of clay flower pots, all different sizes, containing geraniums. We stood in the porch and, before we had a chance to ring the doorbell, Peggy had opened the door and invited us in.

Jack and Peggy's house was a real home. Comfortable chairs of different kinds graced the front room. Many photographs of family members adorned the fireplace. Some of the pictures on the walls had been painted by Pam, Peggy's daughter, and indeed, the artistic trait must run in the family as several pictures obviously drawn by a young child had pride of place. These had been drawn by Gemma, their granddaughter, we were told. Some deer antlers hung from the wall. Of course, we were in Exmoor, home of the red deer.

Peggy busied herself and made us some supper as Jack spoke of his time on the farm. They were a very easy couple to be with and it was so refreshing to be in the company of people who took such pleasure in their surroundings.

After supper, as Peggy and Jack took us out through their back door to see their garden, you could see why they were happy there. Stone steps led down from the back door to a small yard with a small brick wall surrounding it. Every possible vessel from a sink to a barrel was filled with cascading flowers, and yet it was completely unpretentious as the old boots stood by the scraper close to the door and the wire washing line hung across the yard. A pile of logs stacked by the shed were waiting for the return of the cold weather. A path at the side took us down to the tiered garden which sloped down to a field and eventually the stream we had passed on our way up. Peggy showed us the tortoises grazing, explaining which ones lived in different areas of the garden, and Jack took us down to where the ducklings were, now almost adult with their plumage nearly complete. We were amused by their tufted ducks with pom-poms on their heads – all different colours, some with lovely crests right on top of their heads and others where their crests looked more like hats that were slipping off! All around was the view of the Exmoor hills and Jack explained how you could see the deer browsing early in the morning.

It was a lovely visit, and eventually we collected the eggs that we had come for. Peggy had already placed them carefully in a container and covered them with sand, and had been keeping them warm in the greenhouse. Leaving with our precious cargo, we bade farewell with the promise that we would let them know if we were successful.

Once home, the container with the eggs was placed in a tank with an electric light to keep the temperature up and a bowl of water for humidity, and we sat back and waited.

After nine weeks of looking at a container full of sand you get somewhat bored with looking! Then suddenly, one morning, we noticed that one egg had mysteriously appeared above the sand. We did not realize that the baby tortoise inside begins to rotate and this brings the egg to the surface. In much the same way as a chick, the little tortoise with its egg tooth on the end of its nose has to go through the laborious job of breaking the shell. Excited, we watched.

Slowly the egg shell chipped away, and a perfect miniature tortoise pulled itself out on to the sand. To start with the shell of the baby tortoise is soft, as inside the egg they have almost been folded in half, but slowly the shell hardens. The markings are so clear. In our first year we were able to hatch 15 out of 16 eggs and Peggy has kindly given us eggs to hatch most years since, although never have we been as successful as that first year. Sadly Jack has since died, but we still go and see Peggy when we can. It's somewhere that you can relax and be at peace with the world.

It may be difficult to get a tortoise, but it certainly will not be difficult to get a red-eared terrapin. Unfortunately, the importing of terrapins is not illegal and seeing these sweet little swimming 'tortoises', about the size of a 50 pence piece, in the tanks in a pet shop can seem rather appealing. What a pity there is not a notice explaining that these terrapins are going to grow at a phenomenal rate, and within a year you will have a fair-sized terrapin, probably in a tank that is far too small for him. Because they need heat, the smell will probably be unbearable; and it is also quite likely that by now they will bite!

We had one offered to us the other day by a lady whose husband had left her (and the terrapin). She never had liked them, she told us, and she wanted to get rid of this one quickly. It was a large one, she continued; there were in fact two before, but this one had killed the other and eaten most of it – were we sure we didn't want this large terrapin? No, we decided, perhaps not. – Well, who's to say? Her husband could have been just feeding the terrapins, tripped and fallen in the tank and . . .

We have got quite a few red-eared terrapins in a pond in the greenhouse and when the RSPCA rang to say they were looking for a home for one, we agreed to take it. When the inspector arrived, he got a big round tub out from the back of the van, and inside was a large green thing about the size of a tea plate. Terrapin it may have been, but I had never seen one quite like it before.

Until I was able to identify it, I commandeered the bath, much to Derek's disgust. It was obviously more aquatic than the red-ears as its legs were real flippers, and the body was soft. But the most unusual feature was that it could tuck its head into its shell with just its long pointed snout sticking out, or it could extend its neck to up to seven inches, which one can only describe as a distinct resemblance to a phallic symbol. Simon spent quite a lot of time playing with it as it would swim quite quickly up and down the bath following your finger in the water.

We were unable that day to find anyone who could advise us and so it remained in the bath. After a quiet evening watching television, Derek got up and went to the bathroom to get ready for bed.

'How long is this thing staying in here?' came the stern voice as the light went on.

'Just until I can find out what it is,' I replied meekly.

As it happened, Squidgy did stay in the bathroom for quite a few days as we discovered that it was a soft-shelled terrapin (well, well, well!), one that would not be compatible with the red-eared terrapins in the greenhouse as it would probably fight with them.

The lifestyle of the soft-shelled terrapin is to hide itself in the mud or stone at the bottom of the water and, just by extending its long neck, catch its prey as it went past. We were also warned that they can bite and, due to the long-extending neck, there was only one way to hold it and that was from the back – if you held it by the side, the neck was long enough to reach you quite easily! I did not tell the expert that my son had been playing with it!

On hearing about our new arrival, Francis Stothard, the photographer I mentioned earlier, was sent out to get a picture for the newspaper. Lifting Squidgy out of his tank I placed him on the floor in front of Francis as he knelt to get the picture. I stood by, expecting to have to bring the terrapin back if he walked away while the picture was being taken. There was no way that this terrapin was going to walk away from having his photograph taken, even if he did disagree with it happening. Squidgy decided he would charge Francis, with his mouth snapping at the same time. Very quickly Francis was back on his feet, but this did not discourage the terrapin who continued to advance. Coming towards me (for protection!), Francis said, 'He doesn't look very friendly.'

In fact, taken by surprise, both of us backed away. It wasn't until

he had both of us in the corner that we realized the stupidity of the situation, on the defensive against something that could reach no higher than your ankle! With tremendous bravery we sorted out the situation, got the photograph and put him back in the bath.

A second complaint was received from the master of the house the following evening as he entered the bathroom.

'He's not hurting you, is he?' I called back from the kitchen.

'No,' said Derek, putting his head round the door, 'I just don't like the way he looks at me.'

Squidgy was eventually given a large tank all to himself in the dairy.

We hold a tortoise and terrapin weekend at the centre each year when the local Chelonian Group put on a display and visitors can come and see different breeds of tortoises and learn more about them. Some people have had tortoises for years and never even knew what sex they were or which species.

We had two tortoises brought to us one year by a gentleman. One had been his pet as a child and one had been his father's pet as a child, so the ages were known to be at least 60 and 90 years respectively; and as they would have been imported, they would have attained a certain age before arriving in this country. Both of them, through all the time they were kept, were thought of as males – one called Jimmy and one called Binky. It turned out that they were both females.

Visitors come with all sorts of problems for the group to solve, from tortoises that will not eat, to frustrated males that attack shoes!

Hopefully people now having tortoises as pets will be more considerate and offer them a better quality of life than they have had in the past. Certainly, if they have been reared in groups, I don't believe they should be kept as individuals as they are a colony creature and can grieve if on their own.

It was not until I went to a lecture on turtles that I became aware of the effect that we, as holidaymakers abroad, are having on the very existence of sea turtles. We only have eight species of sea turtles, one of which, Kemp's Ridleys, is destined to become extinct by the year 2000 if research cannot be increased in order to save it. All of the species have reduced dramatically in numbers, some by as much as 80 per cent since the 1950s, and are facing eventual extinction.

Very little is known about these large lumbering reptiles that drag themselves on to the beaches of tropical and sub-tropical seas. They return to the beach where they were themselves hatched once they are old enough to lay. Indeed, sea turtles will navigate and return on a regular basis according to which breed they are. Some turtles breed every year, others every two or three years.

When the turtle arrives at the beach, she will go in search of a quiet area, well above the high tide mark, where she slowly digs a hole that is half a metre or more deep. This will usually take half an hour. She will lay 80 to 100 eggs, each about the size of a ping pong ball, into the hole. The eggs are soft so, to make sure they do not break, she will often guide them into the hole using her back flipper which is slightly cupped. Once she has finished laying the clutch, she will cover them with the warm sand. Then, using her back flippers, she throws sand over the area to a distance of several metres to disguise where she has laid her eggs. Then, slowly, she wearily returns to the sea. Her maternal efforts are over.

The eggs are left to incubate in the warm sand and when the time comes for them to hatch out, they all emerge at the same time. Each baby turtle starts an unusual trembling motion with their four flippers. This movement by the hatchlings, which can be as many as 100, makes the sand around the nest shake; the sand particles rain down past the baby turtles which effectively builds up the floor of the nest. The nest floor is therefore moved upwards, almost like a lift, until the babies reach the surface. Usually, the tiny turtles emerge at night and make for the lightest point, which is the sea as it reflects more light.

There are many predators waiting by this time, such as raccoons, birds, crabs and dogs, all ready to make a meal out of the baby turtles, which is why so many eggs are laid. Hopefully, from the clutch laid, half the hatchlings will make it to the sea. Even then life is fraught with dangers. They swim for five days with a natural navigation and then they disappear. No one knows where they go – one can only speculate, but it will not be until they are approximately 18 months old that they will be seen again. Many think that they disappear into the undersea, where it is so dark and deep that we have little knowledge of it.

The taking of eggs and turtles for food is having a tremendous impact on their numbers. Many are killed as an unintended result of our uncaring fishing methods, when it is possible to use equipment that would allow them to escape; but saddest of all is our intrusion on their beaches. Interference is caused by local people who take tourists to watch the large female turtles as they lay their eggs, causing disturbance with lights and noise. Continual walking on the nest sites compacts the sand so that the hatchlings are unable to get above ground once they hatch out. And even if they do hatch successfully, the large modern hotels being built on the edges of the beaches confuse the hatchlings when they reach the surface, and they often make for the artificial lights instead of the sea. The next morning, in daylight, far away from the sea, they die from dehydration.

Education is the way forward. Care for the Wild is one of the many organizations that is funding not only research but training for local people to manage nesting sites and learn how to protect turtle species in their own countries. New developments are being guided as to the illumination of their buildings so as not to distract the hatchlings as they emerge.

Up until recently, we were unaware that leatherback turtles frequent the seas around the British isles in their long journeys for their main diet of jellyfish. Fishermen who caught them brought them home as trophies, often killing them in the process. Hopefully, now more fishermen realize that the turtles cause no harm and are part of our marine life.

We ourselves are all beginning to care for the world around us. Now there are many more possibilities of visiting other countries for holidays than there ever were before. It is an experience that we all hope to have, but it is up to us to make sure that in our desire to see wild animals, tropical forests, coral reefs and other once-in-a-lifetime experiences, we do not destroy the very things that we wish to see by putting impossible pressure upon them.

6

Badger Problems

If you become interested in badgers, then, like me, you will probably become hooked. Become a badger group member and life will never again be dull!

All over the country, there are badger groups which are affiliated to the National Federation of Badger Groups, whose main office is in London. Admit to a badger group member that you like badgers and have some spare time on your hands and you will be reeled in so fast you won't know what is happening to you.

'I don't know very much about badgers' is not a line that is going to help you escape; every group runs training days where you will be taken out in the field and shown tracks and signs. These days can be great fun because usually the members are very knowledgeable in all aspects of wildlife, and you will come home having learnt not just about badgers but about other things as well.

You've got bad legs? Well, that's no problem either because they will tie you to a chair in a hall and give you a slide show – there's no escape!

Every member, whether they have plenty of time on their hands or hardly any at all, will bring different qualities to the group and be valuable towards the success of the whole group. Some people are better at fundraising, others will be able to give talks to groups and schools. Surveying of land to record setts for national surveys, or even for developers, is important too, and the more energetic can be involved in this way. And then there are walkers, who just want to monitor 'their own' setts which they see as they take their daily walks – sort of 'Sett monitors', just keeping an eye on their local badgers.

But beware! – because you will find that as you become more interested, you do learn more about badgers and before you know it, you are 'qualified' to do all of the above and will also be sent out to solve badger problems.

I was reading through the original membership forms of the Somerset Trust Badger Group the other day and found my own application. It went as follows:

Please answer yes or no to the following questions:

1. Are you interested in attending regular meetings? Yes
2. Would you be involved with fundraising? No
3. Would you be prepared to serve on a committee? No
4. Are you interested in giving educational talks? No
5. Would you be able to go out to badger problems? No

Somewhere along the line, I must have forgotten the answers I gave because I now do all of them – so you have been warned! It's a lot of fun, you do learn a great deal (even if you only want to know more about badgers because they feed in your garden), you may be able to get the chance to go on a badger watch – for I'm sad to say, despite the claim that they are the nation's favourite wild animal, they still need protection.

In some areas protection is needed more than in others. The badger groups in Yorkshire have to do a tremendous amount of work to protect their badgers. It is hard to believe that even in this day and age there are evil people who still participate in the sport of badger-digging and baiting. The general public is usually unaware that 10,000 badgers every year are taken for this reason, despite having a law that protects the badger and its sett. This is no figure plucked out of the air: it is based on 9,000 setts found to be dug and recorded, working on the basis of 1.1 animals being taken each time. Of course, sometimes they might get two or three and the next time nothing, but rest assured there are bound to be even more setts that are dug and never discovered.

Eighty per cent of all badger setts in Yorkshire are dug, and because they have harvested the badgers so much the diggers are moving to other areas such as Wales and Gloucestershire; sadly, even Somerset now is starting to get recordings of setts that have been disturbed. The police are very interested in any suspicious actions that may appear to be related to badger-digging. They have come to believe that the sport is drug-related. The badgers are dug up, and pitted against dogs with bets being laid as to how long the badger will last; the money gained from this is then used to obtain drugs which, sold on the open market at street value, can be quite a lucrative business. If any of you see suspicious people out in the country carrying spades, please do not approach them. They can be very dangerous people. Take descriptions of them and note their car registration numbers, if possible, and then contact the police. If they have the manpower, the incident will be investigated immediately. Should it turn out to be a false alarm, the police will not mind as they will realize your good intent and are keen to stamp out this terrible sport.

You tend to think these things do not happen locally. However, only last year, a teacher from the Bristol area brought a class out to visit the centre purely because, from the conversation of the children, the teacher realized that the parents were involved in badger-baiting. He hoped that by bringing the children to us, and by their being able to meet Bluebell our tame badger, he would be able to get across to them what lovely animals badgers were and that they did not deserve to be treated in this sickening way.

The south-west has a very good population of badgers; in fact, 25 per cent of the total badger population of the British Isles can be found in this area. The reason for this is that it is a dairy area with plenty of grass and this in turn means plenty of worms, which are the staple diet of a badger. Badger group members in our area therefore have to accept that, by the very nature of this animal whose lifestyle is to dig, badgers will and do cause problems. As much as possible we go out to problems and try to advise on a solution that is acceptable to the complainant, and hopefully the badger too!

I received a telephone call from a Mrs Squires in Berrow, who certainly sounded to be at her wits' end. Whenever I get a call starting with 'I've got a badger in my garden' I try very quickly to say 'Gosh aren't you lucky!' because this kind of call usually proceeds with a list of complaints as to what they have done.

This time the poor woman nearly went hysterical. 'Lucky! Lucky! You wouldn't believe the damage it has done to our garden. It has smashed through our fence in three different places, eaten 125 fuchsias, made holes in the lawn and some really nasty ones in the flower beds which it fills with poo! My husband and I have lost £400 because we have had to cancel our holidays because of the damage he is causing, and it has got so bad that we dare not go out together in case the rotten little badger creeps in and starts digging everything up before we get back again. We are a retired couple and it is just ruining our lives. My life is a nightmare – an absolute nightmare. I want you to come and take it away.'

Well, I thought, my glib answer had not worked this time. I tried to reason with her, explaining that often in the summer when the food supply disappears, particularly in dry weather, badgers are tempted into well-kept gardens which the householders water regularly, keeping all the worms and insects near to the surface – just right for a badger. My advice would normally be to put out a food supply for them until the weather changed and, with full tummies, they would usually then leave the garden alone. It is also possible to use electric fencing to exclude them. However, because of the amount of damage this badger seemed to have done, I decided it was best to have a look for myself.

Mrs Squires and her husband live on a fairly new development in Burnham. We do get many problems in this area because, slowly, more and more building work has encroached upon the badger territories that were there in the first place and the badgers have had to turn to foraging in people's gardens in order to find enough food. I arrived at the house, as arranged, at mid-morning and Mrs Squires couldn't wait to take me out into the back garden to see the damage. She was very pleased I had come so quickly.

When I got to the garden, it was not what I had expected to see. The garden was just perfect. The lawn looked like a bowling green. Plants were arranged in symmetrical patterns in beautiful curved flower beds which were a mass of colour. Trees and bushes were perfectly shaped, and a greenhouse crammed full with cuttings boasted many varieties I did not even recognize. Here was a couple who dearly loved their garden and any disturbance of soil or hole in the grass was corrected immediately. There was just no sign of any damage other than three strategic holes which had literally been smashed through the lap fencing by this desperado badger.

Mrs Squires was a delightful person, very elegant in her dress and obviously very proud of her house and her garden – and so she should be, for it was perfect. 'He dug a hole here,' she pointed as we walked round the garden, 'and here, and this is where he had all my fuchsias. And he always does one of those . . . those dirty holes right here. My husband has to clear that up, I just can't. I don't care what we do, I don't want him in my garden.' I explained that I could not take him away, as not only was this illegal, but to put him somewhere else would mean putting him in a different territory belonging to another social group of badgers, and they would probably kill him as an intruder.

'Oh, I don't want him hurt, but we have tried putting things down and blocking the holes and he just digs them out again,' Mrs Squires explained. If a badger can overturn a stone weighing more than 50 pounds, more than his own body weight, just to get to peanuts underneath, as has been proved, there is not much that is going to stop a badger who is determined to go a certain way.

'By the way,' said Mrs Squires dropping her voice, 'in case you are wondering where my husband is, he always goes down to the club each morning, only for a half, of course. He should be back soon.'

I really did not want to suggest electric fencing because there was not enough damage for it to warrant such steps. Remembering something that had been discussed at a recent Badger Group Conference that I had attended, I began to explain. 'There is one thing that I have heard of, although I must admit, I haven't any proof that it works . . .' I started.

'Anything, anything,' Mrs Squires said, 'I'll have a go at anything.'

'Well, please don't think I'm making fun but I have heard that if you pour human urine just at the places where the badger enters your garden, you are copying their lifestyle because they mark out their territories with dung pits. Evidently it has been used before and has been found to be successful.' Smiling, I touched her arm and joked: 'of course, it can be put in a vessel first, it does not have to be put direct on to the ground!' I was anxious to allay any fears she may have had of squatting down in her garden to relieve the problem (pun – sorry!). I waited to see how she would take this suggestion. Her eyes were shining bright at the thought that we may have found the answer.

Just then her husband returned. 'Darling,' she called to him, 'this is the lady from the badger group and she is going to solve all our problems. All we have to do is put human urine down where the badger is coming through and it will prevent him coming in. We'll start this evening up here,' she said waving to the bottom of the garden, 'and put it all along here' pointing down the side of the garden – she had really gone for this in a big way. 'Wait a minute', said her husband, laughing, 'you don't know how much we will have by then. I'd better go back to the club and have some more to drink!'

'We could ask the neighbours,' she exclaimed. I had never imagined I would inspire so much enthusiasm and thought that at this point, before being asked to donate myself, I'd best make my exit.

Amazingly enough, when I contacted the couple a week later, the badger had stopped coming in. I refrained from asking where all the urine had come from – they could have lost some friends! – but I have used this recommendation since and, on the majority of occasions, it has worked.

Another problem in Berrow turned out to be far more complex than I had imagined. It was February and a builder got in touch with me to ask if I would go and have a look at a house that was for sale. The house and garden had outline permission for six houses but there were several badger setts on the land and he wanted some advice. I arranged to meet him there the following Sunday morning. Despite having the address, I found it quite difficult to find because the house and garden were so overgrown that, even though I had parked right by it, I still needed to ask a passer-by where it was. The builder had not arrived yet so I took the opportunity of looking around. The house was about a hundred years old. It had belonged to an old lady who towards the end of her life was something of a recluse; she was eventually put into a nursing home and died seven years later.

In her absence, the garden had overgrown and yet there were still signs of the lovely garden that must have been there originally. Rose bushes, unpruned, wove their thorny branches through the surrounding brambles. A privet hedge almost four feet thick protected one side of the house, and huge lilac bushes waved their naked stems full of buds ready to burst once the weather warmed up. Large conifer trees surrounded the bottom of the garden and a tiny forest covered almost one complete side of the large garden. Before I could go any further, the builder and his wife arrived with their children. I had asked Michael Woods, our badger consultant, to meet us as it involved building work and he is more experienced in these matters. The builder had the sale details with him and I was just reading through them as Michael arrived.

The property had now been left to a nephew of the old lady who lived in France and, because of the presence of badgers on the land, he had asked MAFF (the Ministry of Agriculture, Fisheries and Food) to do a badger survey. The survey found that there were eight setts and twenty-one entrances just in the vicinity of the house and garden. The whole place was honeycombed with badger setts, and the main sett was under the house. It had been completely undermined.

As Michael joined us, the builder explained that he really would like to keep the house and the badgers. It would be a lovely place for his children; they could have a pony and he certainly would not bother with the six houses, but in order for him to be able to buy the property he had to prove that the plot was not worth as much as the asking price due to the presence of badgers. Anyone purchasing the land would have to make provision for the badgers before they could do any building work. Was it possible for the badger group to give him a letter explaining the high cost of moving the badgers, or maybe pointing out the risk of disease, so that he could get the price reduced? Michael shook his head. Even losing one plot to provide alternative accommodation for the badgers, there would still be room for five houses to be built and there certainly was no risk of disease.

Seeing that he was not going to get what he was after, the builder left. Michael and I scouted around the place. It was an absolute haven. Although much of it was overgrown, we still found ourselves able to follow the badger paths that meandered over the whole area. A complete ridge of soft sandy soil nearly four feet high was piled on the side of the house, near a tall privet bush, which had been created as the badgers, over the years, had excavated tons of soil. Tree stumps had had the bark stripped where the badgers had used them as scratching posts; lichen growing on trees that had fallen across the territorial paths had been rubbed away by the bellies of the badgers as they constantly used their paths. One path ran down to a small stream where they obtained their drinking water but there were no paths showing on the other side, so they were not crossing the stream. The ivy-covered woodland floor was scraped clear in places and snuffle holes could be seen; these are where the badger finds a worm and twists it as he pulls it out to stop it from breaking off. It was a land of plenty and it seemed as if the house and the garden was a badger territory of its own. The badgers had everything they needed in this area that, up until now, had been forgotten, and everything within it had been allowed to live in peace. The thought of large machinery moving in to clear away the brush seemed such an intrusion, not just to the badgers but to all the other wild creatures that had found a haven here. Even if the badgers were given an artificial sett on the corner of the plot, all the disturbance was bound to make them frightened and in sheer panic they would move away.

'In a way,' I said, 'it's a shame that the builder couldn't buy the house for his family and the badgers could stay.'

'I bet you, if that had happened,' said Michael, 'you could well have found that after getting rid of the badgers, he would put it back on the market for much more than he had paid for it.'

Shocked, I looked at him. It had never occurred to me that

anyone would do such a thing. Sometimes, I am amazed at my own naivety. Michael smiled – he had obviously met these kind of people before. He thought it would be a good idea to get hold of the sale details to make sure that they clearly stated the problems involving the badgers on site. I promised to do this and said I would contact him as soon as I had them. Thanking him for coming, I made my way home.

I had been so taken by the amount of tracks and signs on the site that, the very next day, I returned with two of our students plus camera to take some pictures. Becky and Christopher had only just started at the farm and both were keen on badgers so I left them to roam around as I took some photographs. I kept hearing excited exclamations as they found more and more setts, paths, dung pits and snuffle holes – tracks and signs you would usually have to look quite hard for, but here they were everywhere!

On the way home, we called in at the estate agent and got the sale details. On reading them, I was pleased to see that they had clearly stated the presence of badgers, although quite rightly they had not given the sites of the setts. The agency details even gave the names and addresses for English Nature and MAFF for anyone wishing to gain further advice. I contacted Michael and we both felt that any prospective buyer would be well notified of the situation, and that the present owner, having had a badger survey done and spoken to the legal bodies dealing with badgers, must also be fully conversant with the rules and regulations. We felt there would be no problems. Badgers and their setts cannot be interfered with in any way without a licence. From December to June, licences are very rarely issued except in dire emergencies as this is the breeding season for badgers. Even clearance of scrub close to a sett at this time can be classed as disturbance.

Unbeknown to me, the owner contacted English Nature and asked if, when he came over for the Easter holidays, he would be allowed to clear some of the weeds to make it easier for prospective buyers to see the house. English Nature made it clear that he could only touch ground cover, and that the work was to be kept to a minimum, in order to reduce disturbance.

My next contact was a couple of weeks after Easter, when a very upset neighbour rang to tell me that some men had driven a tractor and trailer into the grounds over the badger setts and collapsed one of the tunnels.

Dropping everything, I drove straight out to the house but by this time the tractor and trailer had gone. I just was not prepared for the devastation I was to see. Sympathetic clearance it was not. The whole area was bare, gone were the trees and the privet hedge – nothing but stumps proved there was ever anything there. The tractor and trailer had been in to take away some of the wood; in doing so the trailer had sunk into the tunnel of the sett. By the main sett which was under the house, and by the other well-used holes, were the charred remains of huge bonfires. Settees and chairs had been dragged out of the house to fuel the fires and the rusty framework was all that remained. As far as I was concerned they knew what they were doing; they had hit the main sett and any other sett that at this time would probably have had badgers. I felt quite sick: how could anybody so deliberately do such a thing? The neighbour came over and I asked her to ring me again if the men returned. I would be back with the RSPCA and I left to make some phone calls.

Both the local inspector and the regional inspector of the RSPCA came and took photographs, and between us we agreed to monitor the area on alternate days. The RSPCA had the problem of tracing the owner and finding out exactly who was involved. As far as English Nature was concerned, sadly the matter had been dealt with by telephone leaving no proof of what was actually said. Our men with the tractor did return, and thanks to the neighbour, I was able to meet the police there whilst they were still on site. Surprisingly, a lot of netting had found its way into the setts, blocking any access back into them.

No prosecution was brought on this case. The law is so complicated that, even though there is a Badger Protection Act, the RSPCA and police are nervous of bringing any actions (which can prove very costly) unless the cases are absolutely watertight.

I returned to this house and garden in early June. Still up for sale, it remained empty. Summer had done its best to hide the scars of the devastation caused in early spring; grasses had sprouted to cover the bare earth, even the roses had bloomed, and the place was a mass of wildflowers, even poppies, with butterflies and insects droning in the warm summer sun. Not everything was hidden – the grey tell-tale signs of the bonfires still remained. The whole area was full of bird-song. It was still a hidden habitat but as I walked looking for the badger setts, I found them overgrown and slowly filling up with debris. No tracks, no badgers – I believe every one of them was suffocated by the bonfires. Who says badgers don't need protection – even in Somerset?

Every year in Somerset, we have a large agricultural show called the Bath and West Show which is held in late May or early June. The Somerset Trust Badger Group have a stand at the show and usually sell goods as well as running a quiz to encourage people to talk to the members about badgers. They will also give advice to people with problems involving badgers.

One of the farmers that came to the stand was Bill Groves. Bill lives at Othery and has a fairly gruff manner. Most of his land is down to corn and he has a serious problem with the amount that gets eaten by the badgers that live there. I think the ladies who had been manning the stall were a little unsure how to take him, and knowing that I was a farmer's wife, they suggested he rang me for advice.

Within a couple of days he rang and explained about all these badgers that he had on his land, and what was I going to do about it? Who was going to pay for all the damage these badgers do? I started to discuss the way of overcoming crop damage – "Tis no good talking on the phone, you come down here and find out just how many of the darn things I've got. Hundreds of 'em, hundreds. If I had my way I'd shoot 'em,' shouted Bill.

'All right then, Mr Groves . . .' I replied.

'Call me Bill,' he snapped.

'All right then, Bill, I'll come down and have a look for you.'

I arranged to go out one evening the following week. 'Meet me by the pub, and I'll show you the fields' he said and the phone went down. The following day we had a badger group meeting, and by chance I mentioned to Adrian Coward, our Chairman, that I was off to see a farmer called Bill Groves.

'Not Bill Groves from Othery?' questioned Adrian.

'The very same,' I said, smiling.

'Well, you surprise me, the last time I went out there . . .' he said.

'You've been out there?' My eyebrows raised in surprise that he needed anyone else to go out again.

Laughing, Adrian said, 'The last time I went out, he told me not to bring that Pauline Kidner woman, the one who looks after badgers, because she is too fond of them! He knows all about you. He's had just about everyone he can think of down there because of the badgers eating his corn.'

117

I began to get cold feet. Adrian's eyes twinkled. 'You'll have a nice time, but I should take someone with you.' I decided to take Derek with me – but I was soon to realize the error of my judgement. We pulled up at the pub on time, and there sitting in the car park on his tractor was Bill. Being of the older generation, Bill had trousers with braces and his shirt rolled up at the sleeves. With his strong arms, brown from working in the sun, he leant on the steering wheel, with a completely straight face. He had a shock of grey hair, and even as I climbed out of the car and walked towards him, smiling and introducing myself, he stared at me with penetrating eyes, merely nodding to acknowledge that he knew who I was.

'Follow me,' he said, and at the same time turned the key in the tractor and its engine burst into life. I ran back to the car but even then, by the time Derek had reversed the car, Bill was already on his way down the road. Catching up, we followed, first down a road and then on to a track towards Bill's cornfields. Eventually, Bill motioned that we would not be able to follow any further as it was too uneven for the car. Getting out of the car, we thought that from there we would walk up together but no, Bill was already way ahead on the tractor and we were meant to keep up!

Eventually he stopped. The tour was about to start – I was already tired! Bill was going to make sure that I saw every badger sett there was to see. 'Hundreds of pounds they cost me, I've had MAFF out, FWAG [Farming and Wildlife Advisory Group], the NFU [National Farmers Union], and no one can tell me who is going to pay. They make these laws without even thinking about it. I'd shoot the buggers, killed twenty a long time ago. That solved the problem and it's what's needed now.' Bill stopped for breath. I quickly interrupted him before he started again with his tirade of complaints. 'Have you tried electric fencing as the crop becomes ripe?' I asked.

'That's no good, it's useless', he replied.

Unfortunately, much of Bill's land was used by the general public, and no sooner did he try preventative measures than the fences would be stolen, and electric fencing is not cheap. He showed us where people had even ridden horses through his growing crop, oblivious of the damage they were doing – it was apparent that badgers and people were Bill's problem. He walked us round the field edges, pointing out each sett. Derek had chatted to him and was beginning to get on all right with him – a little

Catkin takes to the bottle

Catkin again, full up and enjoying a nap in comfort

Baby tame rabbit
(*left*) and (*above right*) three little orphaned wild rabbits. *Below right* a family of baby hedgehogs

One of the prickly babies in a ball

If pigs had wings – our Dotty in flight, with a little help from computer graphics

Hazel the fox cub poking her nose in where she's not wanted

Pauline with Olly, the baby tawny owl

A beautiful little grass snake called Sid

Acorn – always keen on taking a cooling dip

Baby starling with
ever open beak

One of the farm pets
– chinchillas live
a surprisingly long
time and Carey has
reached the grand old
age of 13

too well, perhaps. 'Cor!' exclaimed Derek, pointing to a large sett. 'You've got some badgers here.' 'No, he hasn't', I retorted quickly. 'Lots of holes does not necessarily mean a lot of badgers.' He was meant to be on my side!

As we walked, we found out that Bill lived on his own, and only farmed a few fields now. He pointed out the neighbouring farms and talked about their different farming methods. In particular, he pointed out an old farmhouse on the horizon. 'There used to be a very pretty girl living up there years ago,' Bill recalled. I had a suspicion that, in Bill's heyday, he probably knew where all the pretty girls lived because you could see that, although he was now in his sixties, Bill had probably been a very attractive young man. With his gentle teasing, I could sense, too, that he was not as gruff and abrupt as he would have you believe. I decided that I quite liked him once he had mellowed a bit, and that underneath that hard exterior, he might even be as soft as me. We spent a very enjoyable evening with him despite being taken to every corner of every field to assess the situation, through hedges, under barbed wire fences, wading through overgrown orchards, and meeting up with neighbours who had similar problems with these wretched badgers. However, at the end of the day, we had to agree to differ.

For all the badger setts that Bill had around his field, he had done the right thing: as the spoil heaps spread into his fields, he cleared them away thus keeping them in the ditches. Some of the adjoining fields, that did not belong to Bill, had allowed the setts to spread further and further out into the fields and the setts were now causing quite a problem. Even so, if this does become a problem, the Badger Protection Act does make allowances for licences to be obtained at the right time of year, so that it is possible to move setts out of fields back into the hedgerow.

The main problem Bill had was the badgers eating his corn, and of course, with the general public interfering, it was impossible to use any preventative measures to protect his crop. At the end of the day, Bill could easily be led, through sheer frustration, to get his gun out again. I do wish people would not interfere with farming practices unless they really know the reason for them.

Slowly we made our way back to the tractor, the three of us ambling along as the evening began to draw in and the sun began to set. Bill lazily snapped the heads off the weeds in the hedgerow as he talked about his past life.

Arriving back at the tractor, Bill went on and waited at the car for us. By the time we got there, he was just starting to talk to a lady out walking her dog. 'You're new', he said accusingly. 'I haven't seen you before, where do you live?'

He had such a way with words, so tactful!

Bending over the side of the tractor, Bill nodded towards me and confided in this stranger. 'See 'er, know who she is, she's Pauline Kidner, the one who's always on television' (I wish!), 'the one who wrote a book.' Embarrassed, the lady had to admit she had never heard of me. I laughed and said 'Hello – and you have no reason to know me at all.'

Well done, Bill. He'd managed to embarrass two ladies in one go.

He continued to chat to the lady, whose dog was annoyed that the walk was not happening. Suddenly remembering that I had a book in the back of the car, I went and got it.

'Here you are Bill, a book for you to read.' As I offered it to him, Bill seemed quite surprised. 'When you've finished that,' I teased, 'you'll love badgers too. Thanks for a lovely evening, I'm just sorry I can't solve your problem.' Bill winked and waved goodbye – I bet he never read it!

A couple of months passed by, and when I received an abrupt telephone call, it took me a minute to recognize who it was.

'Good Afternoon, Secret World' – it tripped out as usual as I picked up the phone in the office.

'Pauline Kidner?' said the voice, in a brusque manner.

'Yes,' I replied, trying to connect the voice to a face.

'Bill Groves', came the sharp reply.

'Hallo, Bill, how are you?' I enquired.

'Saw you on television last night,' Bill said gruffly.

'Really!' It was probably what had prompted him to ring, I thought.

'Suppose 'twas a repeat', he retorted.

'It was not', I retaliated. 'It was about hedgehogs – I bet you enjoyed it!' I teased.

'I want to take you out tonight' came the statement from Bill. I was not sure I was hearing right.

'Pardon?' I questioned.

'I want to take you out tonight,' Bill repeated.

Play for time, I thought, this can't really be happening. 'I'm sorry, Bill, I'm already going out, what did you want to see me for?'

'I want to take you down my cornfield', Bill said seriously. I smiled inwardly; most women would be horrified at the offer but I had a feeling I knew what was coming!

'I want', carried on Bill, unaware of my short panic, 'to take you down my cornfield and show you just how much them buggers have eaten of my corn.'

Trying very hard not to allow my amusement to show, as after all this was a serious problem, I said I would go the next afternoon. I was so relieved that I had fleetingly misconstrued his intentions.

'I'll bring my camera down, because I have not seen corn damage before, if you don't mind, but you know I can't solve this problem for you, don't you?' I made clear my situation.

Bill accepted this and once again we arranged to meet at the pub car park. This time his stony-faced greeting did not frighten me; I had warmed to Bill and I knew it was just his way. I followed the tractor as before, but this time once the car had gone as far as the lane allowed, I was allowed to stand on the back of the tractor and Bill took me on up to the field.

Gone were the green stems that had filled the fields on our last visit. Ears of corn, turned gold by the warmth of the sun, waved in the warm sunlight. Snatching at ears of corn, as we walked round, Bill rolled the grain between his fingers to see if it was fit and showed me how it 'cracked' as you bit it when it was ready to harvest. Some of it was ready but there were still areas where the ears were not quite fit; another two days of sun, Bill told me, and the combine could come in.

Where the main paths of the badgers crossed the cornfield, large sections had been damaged. Bill showed me where you could see the tell-tale signs of badger damage as the long stems are pulled down, first with the right paw and then with the left, leaving the corn stems criss-crossed as the animals eat the grain from the ripened heads.

I started to take photographs, including one of Bill in the middle of his cornfield trying to look cross (he was doing quite well really!). As we moved around I took some photographs of the dung pits that marked the hedges.

'What are you doing?' Bill asked inquisitively.

'I'm taking pictures of dung pits, Bill,' I answered truthfully.

'What on earth are you doing that for!' he asked incredulously.

'Well, I can use them in talks about badgers because you can learn different things from dung pits.'

'Just what', queried Bill, 'can you learn from a dung pit?'

'Take a look at this one,' I said. We both peered into the dung pit that was filled with light brown mushy matter (what a lovely subject!). 'This one', I explained to Bill, 'shows that the badgers have been eating earthworms, and there are flecks of black which are the body cases of beetles that they have eaten. You can learn about their diet.'

'Hmmph' was Bill's uninterested reply.

'Now this one', I said, pointing to a dung pit with drier motions inside and flecks of corn, 'shows that they have been eating corn.'

Bill exploded at this rather tactless subject that I had inadvertently got back on to. 'I bloody know they've been eating corn!!' The colour was rising in his face.

'Where was it you said that a pretty young lady lived?' I innocently asked. The subject changed and I got away with it!

We talked and strolled and spent some time making our way back to my car. 'You know,' said Bill, 'if I was a few years younger, we wouldn't have just walked and talked this afternoon.' He winked. I smiled and got into the car, waving as I pulled away. No, I thought, you old rogue, I don't think I would have gone out quite so innocently either!

I meet some lovely characters in the course of my day. However, there are others I have had dealings with that I have never met, nor would I ever wish to – except in court.

One February, I had an enquiry from a young man who lived at Wembdon. For the sake of anonymity, I shall change the names of the people concerned. Stephen lived by a field that was up for sale, and which he hoped he could purchase himself. The farmer who owned the land, Mr Flax, had sold an adjoining cottage which also had the right of way into this field. Mr Flax had therefore decided to create a new access into this field through a disused quarry at the side of it.

Stephen was concerned as in the quarry were several badger setts and, knowing the kind of man that Mr Flax was, he was worried about the safety of the badgers. Stephen asked me to go and have a look and, as a prospective buyer, invited me on to the land to see the setts.

The field had been used for an arable crop and there were several setts all the way down one side of it. Climbing down the steep-sided quarry, it was possible to see that the badgers had used the natural elevation and stone structure to create a labyrinth of setts which covered the whole of the side of the quarry. This was obviously the main sett. Well-worn paths could be seen going from one entrance to another and the evidence of dung pits, footprints and badger hair showed that it was used by several animals.

I explained to Stephen that the badgers and their sett were protected by law and that should Mr Flax wish to build a new entrance to the field, he would not be able to do so until after June, at the end of the breeding season. Even then he would require a licence to move the badgers before doing any construction work. Relieved that the badgers would come to no harm, Stephen thanked me for going out.

Just to make the situation clear, I wrote to the firm of solicitors that were dealing with the sale of the field, stating that I had been invited on by a prospective buyer and had recorded the badger setts on the land. I explained to the solicitor that I had been given to understand that there was a likelihood of a new entrance being built through the old quarry, and suggested to the solicitor that as the badger setts were protected by law, it would be advisable to make any prospective buyer aware of the need to contact either English Nature or MAFF (Ministry of Agriculture, Fisheries and Food) for information regarding the application for a licence. I also mentioned that if they needed any further advice, I would be happy to help them. I received a letter back thanking me for drawing this matter to their attention.

As the Badger Protection Act is still fairly new, we, as members of the badger group, do try to advise and help in development. We are not there to obstruct, merely to help and ensure that correct procedures are carried out to protect the badger and make sure that people involved do not inadvertently breach the law and find themselves in trouble.

I would not have thought much more about this incident had it not been for a rather unpleasant telephone call from Mr Flax, wanting to know why I was interfering. I explained that I had been invited on to the land by a prospective buyer and thought it wise to make Mr Flax aware of the requirements for any further work. Usually a person would call in a badger consultant who would advise them as to the status of the sett, and explain the procedure of excluding badgers from part of a sett, then closing it down so that construction work could continue.

'I suppose you are a badger consultant', was the curt reply from

Mr Flax. I explained that I was not, but could give names of people more qualified than me, who could help him.

'What kind of qualifications do you have to have to be a consultant, then?' he questioned.

'As far as I am aware,' I answered, 'there are no specific qualifications other than experience in the field and knowledge gained from working with badgers over a period of time.'

'How can I become a badger expert, then?' he sneered. I mentally thought that he was the last person on earth I would wish to be a badger expert. Although I had never met him, my reaction to his attitude was that I didn't like him, nor did I trust him.

Answering honestly, I told him that if he wished to join the badger group, he would go on training days where he would be shown how to find tracks and signs. Over a period of time, with the assistance of other members and through dealing with problems, he would gain enough experience to hold an identity card which allows you to advise on behalf of the badger group. From then on, time will give you the experience you need to become a consultant. Realizing that he was not going to get an argument out of me, he abruptly finished the call.

'Who on earth was that?' Derek asked, as he had been sitting in the kitchen listening to the conversation. He had caught the tone of my voice and was aware that it had not been a very pleasant discussion.

'Not a very nice man', was my reply.

March brought in my first badger cub to be hand-reared, quickly followed by others. Before long the usual crazy spring schedule was under way with many orphans finding their way to us. It is a time of year that we all look forward to (except Derek!). When it arrives, we all plough our way through the endless mouths and bottoms to see to, piles of dirty towels and bottles and teats being sterilized in tubs everywhere, with the occasional remark of 'never again!' Then when late summer brings quieter times, you find yourself thinking – however did we manage? And is it ever worth it? But we know that it is and we would do it all over again.

The memory of my conversation with Mr Flax came back, when another young man called Peter rang me in August. He also lived in Wembdon and walked his dog near the field that Mr Flax owned. Peter was surprised to see that wooden gates had been erected in front of the setts and he was very worried that the badgers could not get back in. I explained to Peter that I knew the field concerned and that the farmer, a Mr Flax, wished to put a new entrance into his field through the quarry.

'I expect', I said to Peter, 'that Mr Flax has obtained a licence to exclude the badgers and he will eventually close those setts down, once the badgers have moved into alternative setts, and then he will be able to build his new entrance. It is perfectly legal for him to do that.'

'What if', said Peter hesitantly, 'a certain person has removed those gates?'

Understanding fully what he had done, I said: 'Well, that would be a shame because the idea of a gate is to have them in place for a minimum of three weeks, to make sure that any animal coming out of the sett cannot re-enter. (The gate only swings one way.) But never mind, because whoever is carrying out the licence requirements will be monitoring the gates on a regular basis – daily to start with – to make sure that the badgers do not dig back in or that the gates do not stick. So it will soon be noticed and the gates will be replaced. It just means that the three-week period will have to start again from the time that the gates are re-installed. Annoying but not serious.'

'Oh,' said Peter, understanding his mistake.

'By the way, where did you – or should I say, where did that person put the gates?' I queried.

'Oh, they are in a pile just by the setts. They are not damaged in any way,' Peter assured me.

I was relieved that no property had been damaged. 'OK, well there really isn't anything more we can do,' I replied. Putting the phone down, I wondered just who had been the consultant giving the advice in this case. Being involved with the Somerset Trust Badger Group, I know all the consultants in our area and was not aware of any licences issued in the Wembdon area.

It is always a shame if people inadvertently interfere with licence regulations. I am sure that Peter was acting in good faith, but sometimes fanatical people abuse people's property and rights where development is concerned, which can cause a lot of friction and bring the badger group into disrepute. I could just imagine how annoyed the workers were going to be when they found the gates removed, but then once installed again, hopefully they would be left alone now that I had explained the situation.

Peter rang again at the end of August, very worried. The gates had never been replaced, although two weeks had passed, and he had heard that work on the new entrance to the field was to start the next week. I was very surprised to hear that the gates had not been replaced and began to have doubts about the way that this exclusion was being handled. Supposing Mr Flax had decided to take matters into his own hands, especially after the conversation that I had had with him— ?

I decided to see if a licence had been issued in the name of Mr Flax for the field at Wembdon. If work is to be carried out involving interference with a badger sett the landowner has to apply for a licence. He has to have an independent badger consultant who will oversee that the conditions of the licence are carried out correctly. The consultant should be a named person who has a reputation for badger expertise.

In a situation like that at Wembdon, a badger consultant would go and survey the land where the work was to be carried out. Finding the main sett (which was in the quarry), the consultant would bait-mark to find out the territory belonging to this social group (putting coloured pellets in their food, and locate these pellets later in the dung pits). It would be necessary to make sure that, if the action was to close down the main sett, the badgers would be able to move into alternative accommodation within their territory.

Having seen the land myself, I knew that there were plenty of setts within the field for them to move to. The next course of action would be for badger gates to be placed in front of all the sett entrances for a period of at least three weeks, to allow all the animals inside to vacate the sett. Once this period of uninterrupted exclusion has taken place, the setts should be opened up to ensure no animals are inside before the setts are destroyed and work can continue in the area. The whole aim is to make sure that no animal is trapped alive before work goes ahead.

It is up to the licensing body, be it MAFF or English Nature, to police the licences that they have issued and ensure that the work is carried out correctly. First I contacted English Nature, who assured me that no licence was held in the farmer's name. Then I telephoned MAFF and was again told that there was no licence held in the name of Mr Flax.

If badger gates are placed in front of a sett without a licence, it would be classed as interference and therefore against the law. I realized at this time that I was working only on what I had been told and decided that the best course of action was to go out to Wembdon and check for myself what was really happening. Despite the fact that I was trespassing, if I was going to involve the police, I needed to know exactly what the position was.

It was now Friday morning. Taking my camera with me, I first took a photograph of the day's newspaper as evidence of the date that the film was taken. Arriving at the field, I could see it was much more overgrown than when I had last visited and I had to wade through brambles and nettles. Using the branches of young trees, I managed to hold my footing on the steep sides. There were still the many well-worn tracks where the badgers went from one sett to another. To the left of the quarry, I came across the pile of gates that had been stacked near to one sett entrance. I took photographs of that, and of the setts with the marks in the ground to show where the gates had originally been placed. I also took a photograph of a sett entrance where one exclusion gate remained but where, as the gate had not been properly installed, the badgers had pulled the netting back and were entering the sett behind the gate. All the entrances showed signs of being in use. I also took a series of photographs that included landmarks so that I could prove that the photographs were taken at that site.

I was unhappy about involving the police, so just to make sure, I telephoned MAFF once more, speaking to someone that I know there, to check that there was no licence for this sett in question. The answer was still no. I explained that I would therefore be contacting the police.

At 5 p.m. on the same Friday, I went to Bridgwater Police and asked if a police officer would accompany me to where the badger sett was, as I suspected sett interference. The police were closing down for the weekend and no one was available to go with me at that time, but I spoke to one helpful officer who knew Mr Flax, and he said that he would call in and see him the next day to check if he had a licence.

My main fear at this time was the report that work was to commence the following Tuesday, as I knew that as the badgers had not been excluded, they would still be in their setts. Even if Mr Flax has a licence, I explained to the police officer, please make sure that he understands that he cannot carry out any work until those gates have been replaced and the badgers excluded properly. The police officer assured me that he would. I returned to the farm, feeling I had done as much as I could. I knew, from his attitude previously, that there was no point in contacting Mr

Flax myself. My gut reaction was that there was going to be a problem.

Later that evening, a very apologetic member of MAFF rang to say that they had indeed found a licence in Mr Flax's name – I was impressed that they were working so late in the evening! We discussed the situation and I made clear that the gates were not in place and it was up to MAFF to check that the conditions were being carried out. Could I let the police know that there was a licence issued? I said I would. Unfortunately, I was unable to get in touch with the officer until the next morning, by which time he had seen Mr Flax.

He had been able to see the licence, the name of the consultant and also the dates on which the gates had been checked (!). The farmer also told him that work on the entrance was arranged to go ahead on the Tuesday. 'There are times', said the police officer, 'that you must accept that sometimes there is no point in making a fuss about things. Maybe Mr Flax is not abiding by the rules, but he has to make a living.'

I couldn't believe what I was hearing. 'Those gates, rightly or wrongly, have been removed', I said to the police officer. 'Even the one that still remains has not been applied correctly. I have photographs to prove it. There is every possibility that animals will be trapped underground if work is carried out on Tuesday without proper exclusion. I do not wish to make a "fuss" but if work commences on the Tuesday, my only way forward would be to call the RSPCA out to attend, and the police, as Mr Flax will be breaking the law.' He understood my position, said that I handled the situation sensibly and reasonably, and he would obviously have to leave any further action to my conscience.

I checked with the chairman of our badger group, Adrian Coward, that what I was doing was correct and he agreed. He suggested that I sent a letter to be received by MAFF first thing Monday morning, making clear our worries about the work being carried out.

The whole problem kept churning inside me all over the weekend. I contacted Stephen, who lived right by the field, asking him to let me know if any work commenced. Stephen was going to be away all day Monday but said he would ask his neighbours to keep an eye out for me.

First thing Monday morning, I telephoned MAFF to make sure that they had received my letter. Relieved, I was told that MAFF themselves had been out to take photographs on the Sunday and were now dealing with it. At least now, I thought, with evidence of the gates removed, they would stop Mr Flax from carrying out the work until he had excluded the badgers properly, which after all was only a matter of three weeks. Working through the proper channels and being tactful had paid off.

The urgent telephone call at 10.30 that night told me what a fool I had been to believe that. Stephen had returned home – he had forgotten to tell his neighbours about letting me know about any work starting. Tractors and trailers were working at that very moment, with lights on – they had started a day early. They were obviously keen to get on with the job, to be still working at that time of night.

Frantically, I telephoned the police to meet me there to stop work. They could not get hold of a police officer at that moment and would ring me back. Luckily we have two telephone lines coming in to the centre, so I was then able to try and ring the RSPCA, leaving one line clear for the police to ring back. I tried the national emergency number for the RSPCA for three-quarters of an hour and could get no reply, nor did the police ring back.

I could bear it no more. Asking my son Simon to come with me, we both drove out to the field, leaving Derek to take any message that may come through from the police.

When we got to the quarry, work had stopped. There was an eerie silence. All you could see was a mountain of soil, tons and tons packed hard against the quarry face. Fallen trees with their naked roots had been torn from the quarry face and lay discarded at the side of the road. Every badger that had been in that sett must have been trapped. I felt sick and tears streamed down my face; the sheer enormity of the devastation was overwhelming.

Maybe, just maybe, if the soil is packed against the face of the quarry, the RSPCA could make them excavate down because the soil was against the sett entrances, not actually on top of the sett. Badgers have been known to survive for several hours in similar cases. Clinging to that thought, I returned home and at last got through to the RSPCA. There was nothing they could do at that time of night, but an officer would ring me early the next morning.

First thing next morning, I spoke to both the police and the RSPCA and explained the whole situation. The police officer had arranged to meet Mr Flax with the RSPCA officer on site at 9 a.m.

The police officer asked if I would mind not attending, as Mr Flax had made it quite clear that there would be a breach of the peace if I went. The matter was now in their hands, so I left them to it. I certainly had no desire to meet the man.

When the police officer and the RSPCA arrived on the scene, work had already recommenced and rubble was now being tipped on top of the soil. The police officer asked Mr Flax to stop work: he refused. The farmer was warned that, if it was found that he had committed an offence, he was merely compounding the offence if the work continued. Mr Flax did not care.

The man who acted as the consultant for the licence was present. He was evidently a vet, and as far as I know he is not known for expertise in badger biology. He assured the RSPCA officer that he had looked down the holes and was completely satisfied that there were no badgers down there. Accepting his word, no attempt was made to excavate to the sett entrances. This wonderful vet must have incredible powers that he really ought to share, or even market! If any badger consultant could learn how to ascertain whether there are any badgers down a hole, simply by standing beside it, they would pay good money to acquire this knowledge; think of all the time it takes putting up exclusion doors and monitoring for 21 days, and the cost of waiting all this time.

The police left it to the RSPCA to prosecute; the RSPCA thought that MAFF should be the ones to prosecute as they were the licensing body. I took no further action, feeling sure that some action would be brought against Mr Flax. MAFF, despite my sending them a detailed report plus copy photographs, say there is insufficient evidence.

I am still very bitter about the whole incident. The RSPCA are there for the prevention of cruelty to animals – they took no action. MAFF were shown not to police their licences correctly, and there are growing reports of similar incidents throughout the country. If they are happy with a consultant who can guess whether or not there are badgers down a hole, why put conditions in a licence saying that exclusion gates are necessary? Even the police were unable to take the matter further.

What was it the officer had said? I had handled the incident sensibly and reasonably. Where had that got me? I'd certainly not saved the badgers; I had betrayed the trust that both Peter and Stephen had in me that I would handle the situation. I had failed, and I don't for the life of me know what I could have done differently that would have saved the badgers, or at the very least made someone pay. If I had involved the media at that particular time, I could well have obstructed the course of action of either the RSPCA or MAFF, and it would certainly not have helped the relationship between badger groups and farmers. But at the end of the day, for all my efforts to do everything right – I failed.

As the police officer who attended the incident on the Tuesday said to me, what is the point of having a law that protects badgers if you are unable to enforce it?

We come into contact with many country people, including the farming community, and I can assure you that the majority of farmers are either indifferent to or even protective of badgers on their land. It is only stories such as this one that, when related, give the impression that farmers hate badgers. For every farmer you hear about who pours slurry down his badger setts, or bulldozes over them, there are hundreds that act in a more responsible manner.

The press love to play one side against the other and are quick to make sweeping statements about the voices that are heard. The majority of the farming community carry out their work quietly, wishing for no more than to be left alone to make a living – sadly, they do not make good news and their opinions are never reported.

7

Slugs and Snails and Puppy Dog Tails

We tend not to give our insect life more than a second glance – if they don't manage to get squashed at first glance!

Insects, amphibians and reptiles will usually get the response of 'yuk!' My first involvement with the honey bee made me realize the intricate and brief lives that many of these creatures have and yet how necessary they all are. With the help of local beekeepers, we have been able to create an observation hive where the folds of honeycomb drape naturally within an old log with the bees flying in from the orchard, through a crevice in the old stone wall, to the hive, which is viewable behind glass (the best place to be!).

One can be forgiven for mistaking the honey bee for a wasp as most of us think of a bee as being the size of a bumble bee; however, really they are similar in size to the many species of solitary bees that we have in Britain. There are, in fact, 227 species of solitary bees, 18 species of bumble bees but only one species of honey bee found in the British Isles.

Mr Sydney Lane, a retired teacher, very kindly brought us our first bees. He showed me how to look after them and taught me about their lifestyle. Slightly balding with white hair and moustache, he has the air of a teacher, and keeps the groups of children enraptured by his talks at his bee demonstrations, carefully taking the hive apart and showing them the new bees hatching out and finding the marked queen for them, showing how she is much larger than the rest and is constantly protected by the other bees as she goes about her business of laying anything up to 2,000 eggs a day.

It is only on warm, sunny days that, kitted out completely in veil and protective clothing, Mr Lane can open up the hive, turning the frames, trying to find the queen to show the visitors. With confidence, he handles the bees without any gloves and very rarely gets stung for his bravery. You are told in the books that if a bee crawls into your sleeve or trouser leg, it is important not to panic. Simply turn back the item of clothing and release the bee, who will fly away without stinging; bees rarely sting because, once they do, they usually die. But no matter how hard I try, when a bee gets into my veil or up a sleeve, although these quiet words of wisdom pass fleetingly through your mind, already your natural reactions have you shaking the limb frantically or grasping at the veil trying to squash the wretched thing before it gets you!

I am very lucky in that bee stings do not react on me and their effect is similar to that of a nettle sting, whereas Derek has to be very careful as he can get quite a violent reaction.

A friend of mine, John Callaghan, brought a group of children on an RSPCA outing to the farm and part of their day included a demonstration with Mr Lane. Herding the children into a group, he explained that Mr Lane was going to show them all the bees inside. It was a really sunny day and already there were many bees flying, and as Mr Lane lifted the cover of the hive, bees hovered around and crawled over Mr Lane's hands as he showed the honey in the frame. The children became slightly nervous as the bees buzzed around their heads.

'Don't worry, they won't sting,' said Mr Lane in his usual calm manner, but one or two of the children started to wave the bees away from their heads.

'Don't panic,' John soothed. 'The quieter you are the less chance of getting stung. Just stand quietly.' And he slowly smoothed down the arms of the girl in front. Unfortunately it was just at this moment that a bee became entangled in John's hair: he gave an involuntary scream and ran away from the group wildly shaking his head.

Although he was not stung, it took a few moments for him to compose himself before returning to the group – no one said a word!

One of our visitors did actually have a bee go right down inside his ear and was brought to the first aid post. Despite looking with a torch, I was unable to see anything at all in his ear and honestly thought that he was mistaken. He was quite adamant that this was not the case and we suggested that a quick visit to the local hospital would seem appropriate.

Mr Lane by this time had finished his demonstration and came over to see how the young man was. Peering inside his ear, Mr Lane was unable to see anything.

'Are you sure that it is still in there?' questioned Mr Lane.

'I can definitely feel it in there,' the man replied.

Sure that there was nothing down there, but used to dealing with children that would make mountains out of molehills, Mr Lane pushed the young man's ear close to the side of his head and exclaimed, 'Well, at least that will have killed it, so it won't sting!'

Despite Mr Lane's assurances, the young man went to the hospital and did in fact have a bee removed. Returning to the centre a few weeks later, the young man introduced himself to me.

'Remember me? I'm the one who had a bee in the ear,' he said.

I quickly enquired about his health and apologized for the unfortunate incident.

'I notice you haven't come back on a day that we have a bee demonstration,' I teased.

'I think', said the young man, 'I will give those a miss from now on!'

The queen bee can have a colony of up to 50,000 sterile females that are called workers, and approximately 300 males called drones which actually carry no sting; these are used just to fertilize the queen – and then get chucked out! Although the queen can live for up to five years, the others will live for only three or four weeks, apart from those who live through the winter to keep the queen warm. When a young bee hatches, its first job will be working in the nursery, mending the cells, cleaning and feeding the growing larvae. Soon they will make their way to the entrance of the hive and take short flights, having a practice run at being an adult bee. It is quite amusing to watch them from the ledge, taking off in ever-increasing circles before they finally join in the chores of collecting pollen, water and nectar for the growing colony. In between flights, they will fan with their wings to control the temperature in the hive and keep up the ventilation, and some will even stand guard at the entrance to protect the inmates from intruders.

Bees will travel up to two miles to collect pollen. It is fascinating to watch them return with the pollen bags on their legs laden down with a variety of different coloured pollens depending on the flowers that they have been visiting: from the brilliant orange found in dandelions, through to yellow and even blue when they have been feeding on poppies. If they have found a good source of food, then they will perform a dance ritual once they return to the hive, moving around and shaking their bodies, explaining to the other bees where to find this new restaurant!

A hive with 50,000 bees should make 40 pounds of honey per year, but if you are going to extract this, then you must replace it with sugar water, as really the honey is stored as a food source for the winter when it will be too cold for the bees to fly – with no food they will soon die.

It is always amusing when you find a soul mate, whose sense of humour is similar to your own. I have always had a kind of humour where I can mentally see silly pictures when holding a sensible conversation. A good friend, Michael Woods, has this ability also and it was during a serious conversation with other beekeepers that the conversation turned to the problem of the disease varroa, that has affected many beehives in this country.

As a preventative measure, nicotine strips are placed in the hives to combat the disease; leaning towards Michael, I whispered that I could just see the guard bees sitting on the ledge of the hive having a quick fag, and puffing the smoke into the hive as a precaution against the disease. Very straight-faced, Michael quipped that it would be much too dangerous because of the worry of cancer – much better if they all bought a packet of nicorettes and had patches on their legs to solve the problem. Two very stupid people collapsed in giggles, unable to explain why such a serious subject should cause amusement.

Now I didn't know, until it was explained to me, why the wasp suddenly becomes a nuisance in the autumn with fruit and sweet

sticky things when these items are around all through the summer. The old queen dies and only the young fertilized queen survives the winter, emerging from hibernation in the late spring. She chews wood fibre from logs or wooden posts and turns it into paste to make a papery nest. Once she lays her eggs, she must feed the first brood, but after that the hatching wasps will look for food for the next brood. They kill aphids and caterpillars, using their sting which can be used several times. As the larvae are fed by the wasps, they secrete a sweet saliva which the wasps feed on. In late summer, the queen stops laying eggs and the supply of sweet saliva disappears so the remaining wasps seek other sources of food such as jam and fallen fruit. Slowly, as the weather changes, all the wasps apart from the young queens will die and they will look for a new place to hibernate ready for the next year. I am sure you will feel more sympathetic when that darned wasp appears in the kitchen next autumn – or will you?!

Once we created the observation hive, we had no further use

for the single-frame glass hive that we had used in the past and I decided to use it for an ant's nest, rigging it up with plastic tubing so that the ants would go up and down the tubes to their nest. I had seen the design in a book: all I had to do was to find an ant's nest, and fill the ants into the observation frame along with some earth. They would soon form structures of tunnel against the glass so that people could see the colony busy working underground, turning the eggs and bringing in food; sometimes they even trap aphids in their nest, actually farming them and feeding on their secretions.

First, I had to acquire some tubing and off I went to the local hardware store. I was pleased to find in a 'Do It Yourself' shop that they had all manner of sizes of clear plastic tubing, which was just what I wanted. Asking the man behind the counter to measure some up for me, I hoped he wasn't going to ask me what I wanted it for. He was quite an elderly gentleman who seemed sure that this lady knew nothing about general maintenance, judging by the look of contempt on his face.

'Now what size are you looking for, my dear?' he asked.

'Well, I think 3/4 inch should do,' I replied.

'3/4 inch, you say,' he repeated, 'and how much would you be looking for?'

'Well, I think about 10 feet,' I answered, working out that the ants had to go from the nest, down out through the wall to the ground, and along another piece leading to a food supply.

He picked up the fact that I was not absolutely sure how much I needed. The dreaded question came – 'What do you want it for?' he enquired.

For want of a better answer, I replied: 'Ants.'

'Oh, my dear,' he said, smiling, as he was about to enlighten me, 'you don't need all this, I usually use boiling water.'

'Boiling water?' I questioned.

'Yes, my dear, drop of boiling water on them, that will soon get rid of them!'

'No,' I said, 'actually, I want to keep them.'

'You want to keep ants?' He looked at me incredulously.

'Yes, I know it sounds odd, but I want to create an ant's nest,' I replied.

Having completely come to terms with the fact that I was totally mad, he quickly said, '10 feet you said?' Dismissing any further conversation and carrying the tubing back to the counter he cleared the surface to get the tubing in a bag. The other assistant, of similar age, stood watching.

'I bet', said the man who was serving me, out of the corner of his mouth, to the other assistant, 'you can't guess what this tubing is for? – She', he said, inclining his head towards me, 'is going to keep ants.'

'We get 'em all in here, Bill,' replied the assistant.

I am pleased to say that my ant's nest worked and visitors could lift the sides of the nest and see them working inside and travelling down the tubes to the outside and back in again. The disdain of the shop assistant was only matched by that of the visitors who saw me out with the box, busy spooning into it ants plus eggs to encourage them to stay, and quickly sealing the lid before the little rotters escaped!

We often get things brought in to us that people find in their gardens and are not sure what they are. One of the most frequent of these is the caterpillar of the elephant hawk-moth. It is a very large caterpillar, sometimes measuring up to four inches long. Although its main colouring is brown, it has two large false eyes in the markings and as it is able to swell the front of its body up, it can look quite menacing although it is quite harmless.

We kept one in a tank for the summer for people to see, and then it turned into a chrysalis, having buried itself in the soil on the bottom of the tank, in the same way as it would go just under the surface of the soil to spend the winter. We returned it to the garden to sleep the winter away and hopefully, with the right conditions, to emerge later into one of the prettiest moths that we have, with its delicate pink and brown body with contrasting white legs.

One man travelled for nearly an hour to bring me some unusual insects that he had found in his garden, and that he was sure had escaped from somewhere. We were able to tell him that his grasshoppers were of no danger to him and his family and he could quite happily put them back where they came from!

I would like to learn more about amphibians and reptiles and have just recently joined our local herpetological group – although I don't tell too many people, as it sounds to me more like something that is sexually transmitted!

We recently looked after some slow worms that had been found on the Mendips. People often mistake them for snakes, but in fact they are legless lizards with very strong bodies. They very often use their tails to secure themselves. Slow worms should be handled carefully as, like all lizards, they are capable of dropping their tails; in the event of being predated, they can discard the end of the tail, hopefully leaving them free to escape and the predator with just a wriggling tail! They can regrow the tail but it will not have the fine tip to it.

Slow worms can live a long time, anything up to twenty years and even fifty in captivity. They usually mass together in their hiding-places. Being cold-blooded, most reptiles need to bask in the sun during the day to gain enough energy to hunt and digest their food, but slow worms are seen basking on only a few occasions, mainly just after they have come out from hibernation and again later in July/August. They gain body heat from the reflective properties of stones and discarded tin cans, and can often be found beneath them. The females use their bodies like incubators. Although they lay eggs to reproduce, the eggs remain in the body and the amount of time spent basking in the sun controls how long it takes for the babies to grow. The hatchlings literally emerge from the eggs just as they are laid.

Our two slow worms were called Gloria and Sybil, both the usual 12- to 16-inch body length. Gloria was a lovely golden brown; Sybil had beautiful blue spots on her body which is more common in the male, but it was she who produced six beautiful babies. They were only about three inches long and were a lovely gold colour with completely black undersides. We kept them through the winter and were able to let them go the following spring. It is always useful to have such things to show visitors, as so many people are horrified by creepy-crawlie things that they often kill them. However, if they have the chance to see and talk about these creatures, the more they are likely to accept them.

One of the members of the herpetological society was disgusted when they heard someone describe how they had killed an adder as it swam across their pond after the young frogs. If you have a snake swimming across your pond, then it is a grass snake and it certainly is not going to hurt you. The only defence it has is a foul-smelling liquid that it can emit, and its only other alternative is to feign death.

We were out pond-dipping a few years ago, and surprisingly one of the group managed to catch a grass snake in their net. Everyone crowded round to have a look at it and immediately there was a feeling of regret as the lifeless snake lay on the grass. But then a more knowledgeable member demonstrated that the snake was not

140

dead by placing the snake in an upright position. In order to feign death, the snake then turned its body belly-up, only to be righted again, whereupon once more the snake turned over. The 'lifeless body' was returned to the pond and quickly swam away!

I am lost in admiration for the people who know so much about wildlife, even down to the Latin names that everything has. On such outings there are always the dedicated ones with a magnifying glass hanging round their neck to enable them to identify even the smallest of species found.

I must admit to feeling slightly smug once at a pond-dipping. When sieving through the water dipped from the pond, one person was excited that he had found a particularly rare species of water snail. Everyone crowded round to see if in fact this was so. Dressed in country style, complete with his magnifying glass, the middle-aged gentleman peered at a very tiny dot on the tip of his finger. Undoing his magnifying glass, he studied the creature.

'Do you know,' he stated excitedly, 'I think this is a . . .' and he uttered a long Latin name. Gasps could be heard as, carefully, another member of the group spat on his finger to enable him to transfer the tiny delicate object, and with enormous patience he slowly removed the minute item from the gentleman's finger.

'By jove, I think you're right,' he exclaimed. Another member spat on his finger and, using the saliva, slid the item from one finger to another. Amused at the seriousness of the moment, and at the spittle being passed around, I awaited the verdict.

Silence reigned as he carefully studied the tiny speck. 'No,' he said quite definitely – shoulders dropped – 'It is a duck weed seed!' And he smartly wiped his fingers on his trousers. I was just glad I wasn't asked to have a look at it – spit and all!

There are a few mammals that evoke the shivers and the rat has to be one of them, which is why Dave the rat was treated with respect when he first arrived. He had belonged to a small boy who had been visiting his grandfather's farm, where they were actually getting rid of the rats, but this young lad found a very small hairless baby rat which he was allowed to keep as he wanted to rear it. His parents did not ever think that it would survive, but by being fed with milk from cotton buds, Dave the rat grew into a fine specimen. He was totally imprinted and as tame as could be. Apart from his endearing habit of urinating on you, he was quite a favourite with the visitors and many a brave person had their photograph taken with Dave on their shoulders.

141

Brown rats only arrived in Britain 250 years ago when they stowed away on ships from the Baltic and, once on land, they quickly spread throughout the country. Having come from a cold temperature they were able to adapt much better than the black rat that arrived here from the Mediterranean, and which is now only found around ports. The brown rat can be found anywhere where food is available and for us, with animal feed always around, we must take precautions that their numbers are kept to the minimum.

Dave was not one of Derek's favourites by any stretch of the imagination as he actually has a phobia about rats; when I first came to the farm and bought the children a hamster as a pet, he had nightmares about rats for several days! The main reason for his severe dislike of Dave was that Dave's home was in the nocturnal house and, unnoticed by anyone until it was too late, Dave was busy gnawing an escape route in the corner of his pen.

It was not until Mandy went in to feed him one day that she noticed he was missing. She briefly saw a small whiskered nose poking through a hole in the ceiling. Distraught that he might pick up poisoned bait that is laid around the farm, the girls attempted

to lure him back into his pen with all his favourite foods, but Dave was too smart for that; and when footsteps could be heard in the nocturnal house, a retreating tail could be seen disappearing into the roof.

Dave was on the loose for two whole weeks and it was towards the end of the second week that the earth switch started to throw the electricity off in that area. Only after an ungainly capture, by being grabbed by the tail, which was just not quick enough that time, were we able to assess the amount of damage he had caused.

He had nibbled every single wire, neatly removing the plastic coating at his leisure. Mandy said how lucky it was that he had not killed himself – Derek thought quite differently. The whole of the nocturnal house area had to be rewired. Sadly, not long after that, Dave developed a nasty abscess under his back teeth and had to be put to sleep. Strangely, he is one of our animals that people still ask after, but it is one grave that Derek lays no flowers on!

Bats are another creature that many people have no time for and yet they really are beneficial to have around. Even the smallest species, the pipistrelles, eat between two and three *thousand* insects in a night; they will rid you of all those nasty midge flies that eat you alive in the summer! They even eat the woodworm insect when it emerges so you really should celebrate if you are lucky enough to have a roost in your roof. I do not see how anyone can say they are ugly, especially the beautiful brown long-eared bats that we sometimes have brought in to us. These bats have enormous ears which they fold around their bodies as they sleep. The large ears help them when they are hunting and, as they tend to hunt in trees, they are able to tell the difference between a leaf with an insect sitting on it and one without. I think they look like little flying foxes and find them quite fascinating.

All bats have echo location whereby they emit ultrasonic sounds which we are unable to hear. These are reflected back to the bat from objects in its path and the bat can interpret the sounds into a picture of its surroundings and avoid any obstacle in its way. Because the long-eared bat has such large ears, it only needs to whisper and this enables it to identify textures as well as objects.

The largest bat that we have looked after was Nora, who was a noctule bat. We named her after Nora Batty from the programme 'Last of the Summer Wine'. Nora had a broken wing and would never be able to be released but she coped with captivity very well

– and eat! I have never seen anything put so much food away! We would put special food in a syringe for her and she would chomp away and get quite excited when she knew her food was coming.

Most bats are so small that even if they attempted to bite, their tiny teeth would hardly pierce the skin. But Nora was quite a big girl and one evening my finger was confused with the syringe and grasped with equal vigour. Instinctively I withdrew the digit and the reaction was to shake my hand. Nora was still attached, but the shaking sent her flying (literally) across the kitchen. Luckily I was able to retrieve her unharmed but I was more careful in future!

Mr Mole has to be another mammal disliked by people especially when they 'invade' the garden, although they have probably lived there for years. It is only with fresh excavation due to temperature change that molehills increase. If you were a very rich man, years and years ago, your top hat would have been made from mole skins. They were used because the fur lies flat in any direction. The natural reason for this is that it allows the mole to reverse rapidly when in danger.

The mole is an insectivore, eating earthworms and insects that fall into the labyrinth of tunnels that create their home. Tunnels may be shared by several moles but are only used by one at a time; they are solitary animals, apart from when they meet up to mate. They are very susceptible to vibration and can tell when a tunnel is being used by another mole. This is one of the reasons that some people have tried getting rid of them by sticking windmills around their lawns in the hope that the vibration as they turn will send the moles away – it would certainly give them a headache, I should think! The Ministry of Agriculture, Fisheries and Food even have a 'mole vibrator' (the mind boggles!) but sadly strychnine poison is the deterrent most widely used.

If you have ever seen a live mole, you will have noticed the huge spade-like hands that appear to be attached to their shoulders as their arms are so short. Similar to a badger, they are very powerful in their shoulders, and with very small eyes and no external ears, their main sense is the sense of smell. The mole digs with one limb and, as it does so, it pushes its body against the opposite side of the tunnel which compacts the soil of the tunnel wall. Then turning 180 degrees, it uses the other front limb and pushes its body against the other side of the tunnel. At the same time it pushes the soil that it has excavated under its tummy and then kicks it back down the tunnel with its back legs. After it has dug for a while it turns a complete somersault to face the loose earth, and pushes this all to the surface to create the pointed mounds that we see.

Leading such solitary lives, the female is receptive to the male for only three or four days. Evidently there are no moles in Ireland – perhaps they just weren't quick enough out there!

I have only seen moles on a few occasions, although when they disperse as young adults, they spend a certain amount of time above ground looking for new territory. When I was walking my three original badger cubs, Willow actually caught a mole which shows you just how fast a badger can move if he wants to! It was dispatched very quickly.

We have also had one brought in as a casualty, and it was only on reading up about it that I realized how much they eat. They consume over half their body weight in food in a day. Luckily, the one that came in was only in shock from having been caught by a cat, so we were soon able to put him back where he came from fully recovered! I tried to get some photographs of him but the mole's instinct of disappearing underground meant that my best effort was of its tail!

We often receive telephone calls asking for advice and our staff do their best to obtain the necessary information (which usually means – ask Derek or me). Caroline, who has worked for us for several years and still retained her sanity, was on reception one morning and answered a call from a lady who was upset that a duck was wandering around outside her office. The duck appeared to be looking for someone, she explained to Caroline, and she wondered if it had lost its family. Was there any way we could help it? Placing the call on hold, Caroline got through to me and explained the situation. It was a morning when I was trying to do two things at once, and on listening to the story I was bemused.

'I don't know if it has lost its family', I replied. 'I should suggest that the lady gets in touch with the Salvation Army, that is more their line.'

'Right,' said Caroline, used to getting a sensible answer, and she disconnected to pass the message on. Not surprisingly, my extension immediately rang again – 'I can't tell her that!' she retorted.

'It's all right, Caroline,' I replied, laughing, 'I'm only joking, put her through!'

Needless to say, I came up with a more intelligent suggestion.

You get to the stage where you will believe anything, and when my friend Anne Lees stood looking at me in reception, explaining that she had duck eggs down her bra, I had no reason to doubt her! Anne is one of the Conservation Volunteers in Somerset, without whose dedicated work our reserves would not be the lovely places that they are. The group of volunteers were out clearing some land on nearby Steart Island and, as is usual when strimming has to be done, a couple of volunteers checked for ground-nesting birds before work commenced. Unfortunately a nest of duck eggs was not sighted and it was the strimmer that found them first. Upset at the damage that had been caused, they were able to save three of the eggs, the only problem being that the volunteers had been taken out to the island by boat and left there, and the boat was not returning until the afternoon. Without any further hesitation, Anne slipped the eggs into her bra and spent the rest of the day moving very carefully, and was in fact taunted that it was an excuse not to have to do the heavy work!

Once back on dry land, Anne plus eggs came straight out to the farm and we were able to pop the eggs into an incubator. Amazingly the 'bra babies' hatched just seven days later, none the worse for their ordeal. What was even nicer was the fact that, although at first we had assumed they were ordinary mallard eggs, they turned out to be shoveller ducks which is quite a rarity. Their lovely spoon-shaped bills became more prominent as they grew, and as they were feeding you were able to see the finely ridged edges of their bills that they use to sieve the water in order to find their food.

We wondered about the best method of releasing them, but they made the decision easy for us: once ready to fly they took off – to Steart Island where they were laid as eggs. Just a short distance away when you can fly!

We are so lucky that chance brings in to us such a variety of creatures. Maybe some are more attractive than others but all are equally important to the balance of the world around us.

8

The Kitchen Crew

If you walk into my kitchen in March or April, you might just notice a faint musky smell (I hope it is only faint!).

Our own kitchen has been converted from the old drying room on the first floor of the farmhouse. Shelves line the chimney breast where many, many years ago grain would have been dried. Now the shelves hold ornaments of sentimental value, gifts from my children, friends and parents who have been on faraway holidays: a mask from Venice, a plaque from France, Japanese statues and cut-glass ornaments, all with memories attached to them and given with love. They all have pride of place on the shelves together with the pebbles and dried seaweed that I have collected myself on our holidays at my beloved Lyme Regis. The fact that this holiday is usually taken in November does not spoil my enjoyment as the winter brings a quieter time, with the chance of storms and rough seas with waves crashing over the promenade. Wrapped up against the weather, I find it exhilarating to battle against the strength of the winds along the seafront, only to end up in a tearoom in the town for toasted teacakes – just about a perfect day for me!

The window in our kitchen overlooks the roof of the backhouse and no one can see in. It's my place of refuge, my piece of 'home' that has not been taken away. The whitewashed walls contrast with the pitch pine beams, which still have the large metal hooks where the meat used to hang, although most of the beams now have gleaming horse brasses adorning them. This is the room that we spend a lot of our time in, so two large old-fashioned club armchairs sit one on either side of the small cast-iron fireplace. One of the armchairs is between the chimney breast and the sink, and the hot water pipes run along the skirting board behind the chair.

At this time of year, if you peep over the back of the chair, you will usually see one or two, if not more, small bundles of grey fur curled up in the warm. Sleepy little grunts will be heard until a stretch, or a yawn, makes the bundle uncurl and a beautiful black and white striped face will come into view.

Badger cubs have got to be the most adorable baby mammal ever. Because the badger has delayed implantation, it is able to mate at any time of the year, but the embryo does not implant until the sow becomes sleepy in the winter, usually November/December time. They do not hibernate, but just slow down and use up some of the fat reserves that they have built up through the autumn. This means that nearly all badger cubs are born in January or February.

Born naked, blind and with ears sealed, they are totally dependent on the mother for the first eight weeks of their lives, which are spent underground. They are such slow developers that their eyes do not open until they are five weeks old. It is usually once they come above ground that problems can arise and cubs start to be brought in to us. So often we are told not to interfere in the wild unless we are sure that the creature is in difficulty, but a badger cub above ground, on its own and in the daylight, is usually in trouble.

Our first little badger cub for 1994 arrived in the middle of March. The cub had been handed in to the RSPCA having been found at night on the side of a road. We could only assume that the mother had been moving her cubs and for some reason had dropped this one. I drove down to the RSPCA Wildlife Unit at Taunton to collect it, complete with container and hot water bottle.

The RSPCA Inspector bringing the cub in arrived at the same time as me, so we were able to change the cub over in the containers quite quickly. Colin Seddon, the manager of the unit, came out to see that everything was all right. Colin and his partner Sandra, as a couple, have run the wildlife unit for many years and I have been grateful for all their advice and help. Through their experience and guidance, along with my own observations, I have decided on the ethics of how we deal with the casualties that come into our care. I owe a great deal to them for all they have taught me. They both have a sensible, caring attitude to animals, and will look at any predicament from the animal's point of view. Here there is no personal desire for praise for what they achieve, but a genuine concern for the quality of life and eventual destiny of each creature they come into contact with, irrespective of public attitude or pressure. I admire them both. (It's a shame they're vegans! I once, stupidly, asked them to come for dinner some time, and it took me three years before I could set out a menu that I could cook!)

Colin is tall, a very mild-mannered man (unless upset!), with a beard and an engaging smile. 'How many cubs can you look after this year?' he queried.

'If they are as young as this,' I said, pointing to the tiny cub curled up in her blanket, 'three or four, but after that, Derek might complain!' I pulled a face, and Colin smiled in understanding. We had worked together for some time. When the Wildlife Unit has an overflow of casualties, we are happy to help out and they take from us when we need help. Their unit specializes particularly in birds, whereas I am happier with mammals.

'See you soon,' I called as I waved goodbye, and I was soon on my way home again. It was just getting dark as I pulled into the yard, and, with my precious cargo, made my way to the kitchen. Sitting in the big armchair, I carefully lifted out the small bundle. It was a little sow, and she could have only just been five weeks old as her eyes were still not focusing properly. Chubby rolls of fat showed that she was in good condition, and so were the fleas that were sliding deftly through her soft fur!

The RSPCA Inspector had given her a feed so she was still sleepy, and nuzzling into me with her shiny sensuous nose, she was quite content to lie there. It was nice and warm, and she was soothed as I stroked her tiny head. She was just about the age of my original cubs that came to me in 1989. Her little black and white face wrinkled as she stretched and yawned in contentment. Either side of her head were two tiny rounded ears trimmed with white. Even at five weeks, she had the lovely shiny claws that were going to grow constantly through her life and allow her to dig, an activity which comes naturally to any badger. Lying on her back, the little pads on her feet felt like soft leather.

'You', I said, tickling her black belly, 'are going to be called Catkin.' Not in the least bit interested, she continued to sleep.

Derek came into the kitchen, having heard I was back. He smiled: 'You're happy now, first cub of the season.'

'Isn't she super,' I said, as he looked over my shoulder. Obviously not as enthralled as me, the next comment was: 'Are you going to do something about those fleas?'

The only problem we had with Catkin arriving when she did, was that the very next day we had to travel to Eastbourne for a business appointment. It was only a case of going to the meeting for an hour, but we could not get out of it and we both needed to go. As she had only just arrived, I was not sure how Catkin was going to feed, so we decided to take her with us. She took a little bit of milk through the first night but was not drinking as well as I hoped, so I was pleased we were keeping her with us.

It was an early start the next morning with a four-hour drive in front of us to arrive in Eastbourne at 10 a.m. Taking Catkin with us meant extra arranging of feeding bottles, of nappy wipes and towelling to toilet her, and thermos flasks for hot water bottles to keep her warm. But eventually we were ready, Derek driving and me with my 'baby' in the back of the car with all the requirements.

Keeping to three-hourly feeds, Catkin started to drink more strongly and, half-way through our journey, she passed a motion for the first time. It may sound silly to get excited about this, but once an animal starts to feed well and pass motions normally, you are in with a chance of being able to rear it. 'Oh! lovely,' I called from the back of the car, 'Catkin's been to toilet.'

'I'm so pleased,' came the dry reply from the front.

We arrived in Eastbourne in time for me to give Catkin another feed before our meeting. When badgers are as young as she was, they are just like small human babies and once they have had their feed they fall asleep. So, with her snuggled to a fresh hot water bottle, we were able to leave her asleep in her box in the car while we had our meeting.

Within an hour we were out again and on our way home, but Derek and I were both feeling quite hungry ourselves by then so we decided to look for somewhere to stop for a meal. We eventually found a roadside cafeteria and Derek pulled in.

'I'll have to give Catkin another feed before we go in,' I said, as she had just begun to stir.

Derek wanted to telephone the girls at home to make sure they were getting on all right with all the animals, so he went on in, and I said I would follow once Catkin was full. After ten minutes I had nearly finished, but Derek came back to wait in the car for me. 'I've explained to the waitress that we're going in for something to eat in a minute, but I said that you were just feeding the baby in the car – I didn't tell her it was a badger,' Derek said, sometimes bemused with what he has to put up with.

Soon Catkin was asleep, and leaving her tucked up in the car, we ran across to the café as it had started to pour with rain. Recognizing Derek from before, the waitress waved us over to the table that she had laid ready for us – one chair either side of the table and a highchair ready for the baby! I left Derek to explain that one.

Parents and 'babe' managed to get home without being any the worse for their long journey.

151

I noticed in the next few days that Catkin was very difficult to toilet as her motions were very loose. When I spoke to the RSPCA Inspector who had collected her, he also had noticed that she 'leaked' very easily. We had her checked with the vet and the conclusion was that she had a relaxed bowel; hopefully, in time, the muscles would improve and she would eventually be able to control her motions.

This left us with a delightful badger cub who, on waking up, would walk around leaving yellow puddles behind her unless you could toilet her straightaway. It was absolutely imperative that when you picked her up to toilet her, all towels, tissues and cloths were to hand. There was, unfortunately, no need to stimulate her to empty her bowels by wiping her with a damp cloth; just by picking her up, the pressure on the sides of her body was enough to transmit the message about letting 'it all go'. This did lead to some embarrassing situations, especially when visitors saw her and their immediate reaction was to pick her up and say how lovely she was – which was then very quickly followed by a completely different attitude to her, once they had been doused in 'yellow yuk'!

Once I was looking after Catkin, I was interested to see what reaction I would get from Bluebell as I knew she would smell the young badger on my clothes. At that time she was enclosed in the observation sett, as we had just integrated two sow badgers with her. One sow was our own small badger called Snowdrop. She was brought in to us in June two years previously as a road traffic casualty, and took many months to get better. Then, to our surprise, the following spring she gave birth to twin cubs, having mated prior to the accident; with delayed implantation, she had carried the embryos despite all her trauma. Her cubs went off for release with the cub group of the season, but Snowdrop, I felt, was not capable of coping in the wild without monitoring so I felt she was better off going in with Bluebell.

The other sow, Clover, came from Norfolk and had no territory to return to. As she arrived in the winter at the RSPCA, and they had no other badgers in captivity, it was better for her also to be put with Bluebell rather than being kept on her own in a pen.

All three badgers integrated well together, and it was just a matter of time, as they adjusted to their new home, before we could open the badger gate out into our homeground, and thus give them the freedom to come and go. Blue did not mind not being able to come up to the house as she slowed down a lot at this time of year, and I would keep up contact with her by spending time with her in the evenings in the observation sett.

Going down that evening, I went into the education room and opened the door between the viewing area and the chambers as I usually do. Climbing out at the back of the sett on to the boards that line the tunnels leading out to the enclosure, Bluebell had a good shake; the sound of scratching followed before a final shake as she made her way out to me. Sitting on the floor, I waited for her. Her face peered around the door, sniffing the air. Vocally greeting me, she made her way across the floor and then turned and backed on to me to mark me with her scent gland to show that I was an accepted member of her group.

I ruffled her fur and she flopped on her back and squirmed, using the roughness of the cement floor as a back-scratcher. Rolling over, she shook herself, and then came and started to sniff my clothes. Intrigued with the new scents, she checked me all over and then sat beside me, quietly listening for any sounds from outside.

Running my hand down her back, I scratched her between her shoulders and she in turn nibbled her teeth down my sleeve in a preening action. I pushed her over on her back, and prodded her with my fingers to encourage her to play-fight.

'I have got a little badger cub, just like you were when you first came,' I said as I teased her, pulling at her front legs. Bluebell played, gripping my arm with her front legs and mouthing my hand with her teeth. I had complete faith in her, and she in me. Our relationship had depths that I never realized until later.

I wondered how she would react when she eventually met the cub, but that was some time away yet. She certainly had not objected to the scent of Catkin. Time passed easily as we just sat together, sometimes playing, sometimes preening, often just sitting together. Then, once she had had enough, Bluebell would make her way back to the sett door, glance back and then jump back into the chamber with the other badgers and settle down. I had been dismissed!

A couple of nights later, we were called out to a badger in a barn. He was stowed away behind some hay bales, and the owners had seen him there and noticed an injury to his back. The farm was only a couple of miles away and Mandy, our animal supervisor, came with me.

I usually take a cage and blankets, net and dog grasper to cover just about all eventualities! I don't like using the dog grasper because I feel that it stresses the animal, but on this occasion, when moving the bales would just encourage the badger to run away, it would be easier to grasp him by the neck securely and then move the bales and quickly lift him into a cage.

As we lifted him into the cage, it was obvious that he was suffering from typical territorial bite wounds. These are injuries inflicted by other badgers who have either rejected the badger from their own social group, or have encountered a strange badger that has dispersed from his social group and is looking for a new territory. Wandering into a territory owned by a different social group of badgers can be a dangerous business.

Matted hair soaked in blood covered one ear and, from his middle back to his tail, a large gaping wound, oozing with pus, showed that his injuries were old and infected. Despite all this, he was making it quite clear that he objected to what we were doing and a snarling, spitting badger threw himself around in the cage, with a deep guttural growl every time you went near. This sort of behaviour does make you think twice about picking the cage up, for although the handles are on top and it is impossible for the badger to get hold of you, what with the violent attempts at retaliation, and the noise, all your instincts are telling you that it's not a good idea as you go to grasp the handles!

We took him straight through to Bridgwater and left him with Mark, a new vet at our surgery. It was going to need an anaesthetic before Mark could really do a clean-up job, so I said I would ring later.

A couple of hours later, I rang to see how the badger was. Mark explained that he had cut the rotting flesh back to the healthy skin and it was now going to be merely a question of time to allow the wound to heal. It was a fairly old badger, he thought, judging from the condition of his teeth. My heart sank a little at this news, because normally if it is an old badger with territorial bite wounds, we will usually put them down; for such wounds mean that they have lost their order in the social group, and it is sadly nature's way of finishing off the old members within the group. It is likely that, if you get them healthy and return them to their territory, they will be attacked again. Still, now that Mark had done all the work on him, it seemed fair to give him another chance.

I went and collected him from the vet's, having first put on the heat lamp in one of our care pens and placed a fresh blanket under the lamp to start to warm. We usually put badger casualties on a blanket when they first come to us as it gives us the chance to monitor urine and faeces that can so easily be absorbed in straw. Mr Boar Badger was quieter when we got home, and gently placing the cage in the pen, I tipped it on its side and allowed the badger to climb out. He did not look that old, so I hoped we had done the right thing. He had a scar to his nose that gave him a slightly comical face and, instead of the usual black shiny nose, he had pink blotches. Watching me warily, he sniffed the blanket and I slowly withdrew from the pen. Gently closing the door, I looked through the viewing window at him. He had made his way to the water bowl and was having a drink. Already some food had been put in for him by the girls, ready for his return, so I left him in peace.

Walking down on my usual visit to see Bluebell, later that evening, I checked on him. Despite the large wound to his rump, that seemed even larger now it had been cleaned, half the food had gone and he was lying enjoying the warmth of the lamp. I'm sure the wound must have been very sore but at least it now looked pink and healthy. Badgers seem to have an enormous ability to withstand pain. You're safe for a while, old fellow, I thought, but you are going to take time to heal.

Within two weeks, another badger cub arrived. This one had been found in Glastonbury and taken to a veterinary surgery, where he was placed in a cage with some cat food for the night. Looking rather sorry for himself, the little badger cub was quite hungry when he arrived as he had not yet been weaned and was probably quite confused by the cat food! Here was a chunkier cub, a boy who, despite only being six or seven weeks old, was a real bossy-boots; it was probably his go-getting nature that had led him into going further than he should have done on his own, ending up lost.

Placing him on the floor by the chair, he scuttled behind it where he found another little cub curled up in the warm blanket. Catkin was sound asleep, and despite the nudging of the cold nose of the new cub, she remained oblivious to him as he settled beside her, and he too went to sleep. It was not until hunger aroused her that she met her new mate.

Acorn, as I called the new cub, woke up as well and on seeing Catkin going in search of food, followed behind. Coming towards me, he greeted me with the lovely 'uv-vuv-vuv' sound that they softly purr to one another. He was a very vocal cub and was to become the king-pin of the cub group. Catkin rolled on her back and pushed her two front paws into his side in play, making sure that the new arrival would not give all his attention to me. Pushing her hard with his nose, Acorn snapped at Catkin and tugged at her ear. Standing back in surprise, Catkin waited for a mere few seconds before advancing again to get Acorn to play. This time Acorn was happy to oblige, having made his point as to who was the leader.

Mopping up the yellow puddles that had appeared in this activity, I set about toileting them both and feeding them. (Next time I get new flooring for the kitchen, I have decided to go for yellow – it won't look so horrendous first thing in the morning when you get up!)

Acorn was easy to feed, and with the incentive of another cub constantly nudging at the bottle to get her fair share, the sucking of the teat became quite a serious business. Once the feeding was over it was playtime, and even with cubs at this age, this can be a painful event. The lifestyle of biting and fighting starts here, and although it is only mock fighting, humans do not possess that thick rubbery skin that badgers do, and so quick reflexes are a must.

When you tweak their ears, they show an instinctive reaction of twisting their heads and barging with their strong shoulders against your hands. Once I had had enough, I put them down on the floor to tire each other out. They tussled with the rug and tugged at an old shoe before slowly returning behind the chair. The bedding was sorted out; nosing it up at one side and digging at it with their paws, they finally decided that it was the right shape and, snuggling together, they were soon asleep. Peace for another three hours!

Two badger cubs were fun to have around, but they were soon added to. Sorrell was another male cub brought in three days later. He was found dehydrated on a bridle path at Weston. He was as small as Catkin and was another to be bottle-fed. One week later Tansy arrived, another male, but he was already weaned so he was easier to look after. I was up to the four cubs that I said I would take.

I had never had as many cubs in one season, and it was the same for other cub rearers as well. The winter had been a very wet one, and I am sure the sows were able to find plenty of food and therefore produced enough milk for most cubs to survive to the age when they started to emerge. Then when April arrived, Nature became cruel and we had drought conditions. Most of the cubs were now at the point of weaning, and their mothers' milk was starting to dry up. Now was the time for them to find earthworms and beetles in their foraging forays. The hotter and drier the weather became, the more impossible it was for these young cubs to find any source of food. Slowly the weaker ones became dehydrated and, unless fortunate enough to be found, they died. Even the adults were finding it incredibly difficult to find enough food and, having to increase their foraging range, more were being knocked over on the roads.

Meanwhile, most of us humans were enjoying the early summer and soaking up the long weeks of continuous sun, completely unaware of the pressures on wildlife. Long periods of any kind of weather, be it rain or sun, can be disastrous to many species.

Even Mr Boar Badger, who was now completely healed, could not be released until we had some rain and food became plentiful again. His wound had taken even longer than expected to heal as the sides would not scab over, so eventually it had been necessary for him to return to the vet for it to be stitched. Stuart Murray, the New Zealander who was our new vet, had been on a routine visit when I asked if he could take the stitches out.

'You'll have to anaesthetize him first,' I warned.

'No I won't!' he said breezily.

We both went into the pen. I covered the badger with the blanket and he appeared quiet, but I have, on many occasions, seen these circumstances change very quickly. 'Just hold him there,' Stuart said gaily, and lifting the part of the blanket that was covering the badger's rump, he snipped away.

My 'end' was growling quite fiercely and I was quite relieved when Stuart said, 'All done.' We both retreated quickly, complete with blanket. The door just shut before the badger hit it.

'Phew!' exclaimed Stuart in his nasal accent, 'I kinda thought he might do that.' And he wiped his brow with his sleeve.

'You sod!' I swore, 'you had no more confidence in the situation than I did.'

'Well, I was quick, and we got away with it,' and he winked.

'Ohhh!!!' I clenched my fists.

When the RSPCA rang to ask if we could take another badger cub, it did not seem fair to turn the cub away, particularly as it was a female and, at that time, we had quite a few boys. Dandelion was found with her sibling, but sadly he had drowned in a nearby stream. It seemed either as if both of them had strayed or maybe the mother had been killed and they had started to wander to find food. Dandelion was another cub that was already weaned on arrival. Her coat was very fluffed up and she looked like a large powder puff. She was fairly nervous, but soon joined the rest of the cubs.

The final cub to come and join the 'kitchen crew' was Rosebud. We have a local couple, Mr and Mrs Reddish, who monitor the badger setts that are near to their home. On this particular morning, Ray was in the garden and a neighbour, who had been walking his dog, called over to him that there was a dead badger further down the road. Ray immediately put down his spade and walked back down the road. He was sad to see that a large sow badger had been knocked over on the road, but despite her injuries, she had dragged herself back to the entrance of her sett. Having used all her strength trying to return to her home, she had died.

Ray had a look at her and discovered that she was a lactating female. He immediately realized the seriousness of the situation and decided to watch the sett. There was every reason to believe that one or more badger cubs were down in the sett, and with their mother killed, hunger would soon entice them to come above ground to find a food supply. First Ray telephoned us, and Derek went out to see what the situation was. Ray and Doreen's son, Paul, had also arrived by the time Derek got to their house. All three men, Derek, Ray and Paul, went to have a look at the dead badger and as they neared the sett, a small badger cub was seen with its head poking out of the entrance. Sensing the arrival of the men, despite them stopping in their tracks, the cub disappeared back underground.

They decided to leave the corpse of the mother just away from the sett, in the hope that the cub might emerge and try to reach it. Ray, a local beekeeper, had a meeting that afternoon, so Paul offered to stay and watch, although realizing that only with a lot of luck would he be able to catch an agile and very frightened badger cub.

A jubilant Paul arrived at the farm only a matter of three hours later, complete with the cub, that they had named Rosebud, contained in a box. He had managed to catch her as she had hesitantly emerged, trying to reach the still body of her mother, not understanding why she had not returned to their chamber where usually, at this time of day, they would have lain together, safe from the outside world.

Rosebud was shivering with fear, surrounded by human voices.

In the daylight, this was not a world that she recognized and she did not like it.

Taken upstairs, once she was de-fleaed, she was introduced to the badger kitchen. Slowly, I managed to slide the blanket that she was sitting on out on to the floor. Spitting, she made all her hair stand on end, making every effort to appear as large as she could. Back arched, she sidled by the kitchen unit. I started to talk softly to her and of course, hearing my voice, the rest of the crew woke up. Acorn was the first to inspect the new arrival, followed by Catkin and Sorrell. Rosebud allowed herself to relax but she still watched warily all the new faces.

By this time all the cubs had been weaned and they were all quite individual personalities. Catkin and Acorn had hair loss, which is quite common in hand-rearing but it does nothing for their appearance; indeed Catkin, who was almost completely bald, resembled a Vietnamese potbellied piglet except for her black and white striped face. They all tumbled out from behind the chair, Tansy and Dandelion being the last as they were slightly more nervous. As these two were already weaned when they came in, there was no need for me to pick them up; and although they would come and play if I sat on the floor, they were very wary of anyone just walking in the room. Indeed, if the door opened quickly when they were out playing, they would run spitting behind the chair. It may sound unusual, but these are the reactions you are hoping for if these little cubs are going to go back successfully into the wild.

Rosebud surveyed the scene, and sniffed at Acorn who was giving her his usual welcome; then, sidling further past the armchair, she saw the fireplace. Jumping into the fire basket, she disappeared up the chimney! Luckily the chimney is blocked off and therefore the fireplace is for decoration only. I decided that the best course of action was to leave them alone to sort themselves out. Quietly shutting the door, I went downstairs to see to the visitors.

I returned half an hour later, to check that all was well. I tiptoed in, so as not to disturb them, as a mealtime was not yet due. The heap had returned behind the chair. I could just make out that the pile consisted of five cubs, Acorn, Catkin, Sorrell, Tansy and Dandelion. No Rosebud. Peering up the chimney, I could see a very sooty face peering back at me. Rosebud, having found a ledge just above the firegrate, had not come down from her hiding-place. Time would sort things out, I thought, and I again left the kitchen in peace. Hardly any of the noise from downstairs carries up to the kitchen, and with the light off it is a fairly dark room. Just the gurgling of the water pipes and the gentle hum of the fridge break the silence. Small wonder that the badger cubs take to it as a haven, as I do.

If it were not for the dedication of people such as Ray, his wife Doreen and son Paul, who quietly care for our wildlife in their everyday routines by watching and being prepared to help when situations occur, then many more of our creatures of the countryside would suffer.

Ray went back to the sett later that evening and watched all through the night and again the following evening, just in case there was more than one orphaned cub. No other cub emerged, so we hope that it was just a single cub.

It is often rumoured that badgers bury their dead by taking a corpse below and blocking off a chamber which is then not used for many years. I have no evidence of this, but the following evening the body of the dead sow disappeared. I wonder if other members of the family group took the body down into the sett and buried her there?

Ray Reddish has saved not only a badger cub but a swan as well! Not so long ago, when a cygnet was caught on a fishing line which had become trapped on an overhanging tree on the far side of a lake, Ray came to the rescue! The cygnet had swallowed a fishing hook and the bait and now, with the line caught in the tree, it was frantically thrashing around in the water. The RSPCA had been called but as yet had not arrived and Ray could see that the cygnet was going to do a lot of damage unless the line could be untangled.

Despite not being a particularly good swimmer, and with the lack of any other means of getting to it, Ray commandeered a car tyre. With a rope secured to it, so that he could be pulled back by the other observers (who were not prepared to go in!), Ray took the plunge. It was really quite a dangerous thing to do, with the mother swan being nearby and the unknown beneath the surface of the water. He was able to reach the cygnet and break the fishing line, leaving enough to dangle from its mouth so that the hook could be located. Then leaving the cygnet to float in the water to get over the stress of his accident, Ray returned to dry land. When the RSPCA finally arrived they were able to catch it up and take it back to the wildlife centre to recover. A very wet

Ray squelched his way home, where his heroics were played down by a telling-off from his wife!

Six badger cubs in the kitchen – and my husband still had not left me! Even I had to admit, it was a lot of work. As soon as badger cubs wean, being fastidiously clean they usually decide where they are going to go to toilet – basically, where the dung pit is going to be. This year it was to be by the dog basket, so at least we could be prepared with plenty of newspaper laid ready in the locality. Catkin was a little bit different. She in her little explorations had found that us humans, when in need of a 'dung pit', would go down our long hall to the toilet at the end. If it was good enough for us, it was good enough for her, and visitors were amused when this little cub would scratch at the kitchen door to have it opened for her. Waddling down the hall, she would go in to the toilet where the door is always left ajar. Right in behind the door she would go, naturally for privacy – and the pool of yellow would begin to appear under the door and it was time to get the disinfectant out again! She would then waddle all the way back and flop straight on the other cubs who were usually still sound asleep. Maybe because she was the first of the season, or perhaps because she was so small, I had a special affinity with Catkin.

The older they became, the more boisterous the play, and strategic bricks and stone animals were spread around the kitchen in a vain attempt to keep the lino on the floor. In the evenings,

when the visitors had gone, I would leave the door open at the top of the stairs and they would scamper out into the garden for a game before charging back upstairs. Joanne Richardson, a very talented artist who used to be at our centre, helped me on many evenings in order to keep a check on them as they went in all different directions!

Feeding time became horrendous as the art of eating solid food takes time to acquire, and sticking one's nose in the food and blowing bubbles, walking in it and sitting in it are all part of the 'learning curve'. Believe it or not – they don't have dishes in the wild, so cubs can see no reason why it isn't easier to empty all the bowls on the floor and just grub around! I washed my kitchen floor at least five times a day. When friends came up and admired the sleeping 'badger pile' behind the armchair in a nice tidy kitchen, they were completely unaware of the mess that erupted once they were awake – although Derek did try to enlighten them with quite graphic details at times!

One evening I noticed that it had been very quiet for about ten minutes when previously they had been charging up and down the hall playing with a ball. The door down to the garden was closed so I knew they were not out there, and no one could be seen in the bathroom, although they are quite capable of falling asleep under our old-fashioned enamel bath which is on legs. I went in search of the missing six!

As I neared our bedroom, I could hear from the whickering that they were having a whale of a time. We, at that time, were sleeping in our son's bedroom while he was away, as we were having our bedroom decorated. All the furniture had been stacked against the wall, including the mattress from our bed. As I opened the bedroom door, lots of little grey bodies scuttled behind the pile of furniture, spitting as they ran, frightened by the sudden entrance of a human. The cubs had managed to pull over the mattress, which was made of foam, and, starting from the middle, they had scratched and dug until the centre of the mattress was no more. Various sized pieces of yellow foam covered the floor. 'What have you been doing!' I gasped, and knelt on the floor, at which Acorn, recognizing the voice, emerged triumphantly holding a piece of foam that was nearly as big as him. Sorrell dashed out, grabbing the foam trophy and bowling him over, and then they were all out, tumbling about, excited like children playing in snow.

Quickly finding a bin liner, I gathered up all the evidence (as you can imagine, with a great deal of help from the cubs) and carefully leant the mattress back against the furniture and draped a sheet over the offending hole. By now the cubs had drifted back to the kitchen, worn out from their game, and were soon asleep behind the chair.

When Derek came in for his supper, he found me looking at my catalogue. 'What are you after now?' he mused.

'Oh! I was just looking at the mattresses. You know how I have trouble with my back, and our mattress is quite an old one. I thought it would be a good idea to get an orthopaedic one, while we are sorting out the bedroom,' I casually remarked.

Derek nodded his head. 'Good idea,' he said.

The next day, in the evening, as we sat watching television, I just mentioned: 'You'll never guess what those badger cubs got up to today.'

'No, what was that?' he asked.

I told him about the mattress. 'Wasn't it lucky we had decided to have a new one anyway?' Lucky indeed!

The last escapade in the house before they finally went outside had me being rudely awakened at 3 a.m. by our burglar alarm. Luckily, Derek manages to sleep through that, and I got up. Pulling on my dressing gown but not waiting to put on my slippers, I quickly went barefoot to the master unit and switched it off. I could tell from the panel that there had been a tamper on the circuit in the kitchen.

Opening the door to the kitchen, I switched on the light and the strip light flickered into action. Yet again the scurry of guilty bodies sounded as they disappeared behind the chair. I shan't ever forget the sight before my eyes. My God, had they had a party! Someone had managed to open the cupboard door where we keep all the biscuits and the cakes, and packets were strewn everywhere. They are evidently not into marzipan cake as this had not been eaten but had been ground into the rug and chair covers instead.

Having got the hang of opening the cupboard, they had also managed to open the fridge and only the top shelf had been saved. Two packs of tripe that had been in there defrosting in containers, along with bacon, cheese, lard, butter and paté, had been smarmed over the kitchen floor or partly devoured. Then as a final *pièce de résistance*, someone had managed to chew through the burglar alarm wire. Slipping in, I closed the door behind me and stood with my back to the door, willing Derek to continue sleeping.

Slowly, I set to, pulling off chair covers, picking up wrappers and attempting to make some order of the chaos. Of course, the 'kitchen crew' thought this was part of the fun, and not only had this person come to join in but she had lovely pink toes completely unprotected. This, I can honestly say, was the closest I got to thinking about strangling them! Thankfully they soon began to tire, and I was able to clear and eventually wash the kitchen floor without any 'assistance' whatsoever. I worked my way towards the door and by the time I had arrived there, the soles of both my feet were caked in a layer of biscuits, butter and other edible items that now not only looked but felt disgusting as it squidged between my toes. I was able to tip-toe to the bathroom, to scrape this offending layer off before washing my feet. Having cleaned both the kitchen and myself up, I returned to bed. As I slipped quietly between the covers, the body that shared my bed never stirred.

The next day was a very quiet day. None of the cubs seemed particularly hungry and they all gave the distinct impression that they had tummy ache – I was not at all sorry for them. For the next few nights we barricaded the cupboard doors and the fridge.

There had been so many orphan cubs that season, it soon became apparent that there were not going to be enough release sites. We had two years previously used our sett as a release site, with

My God, had they had a party!

164

Bluebell as an adoptive parent, so we decided to do the same again this year. This was no different than if Bluebell had had cubs herself. Young would have grown up and dispersed quite naturally.

Relieved that at last the cubs were coming out of the kitchen, we shut down part of the observation sett and moved the cubs down alongside Bluebell and the other two sows. For a period of time, the sows were able to have visual contact through wire to the cubs but no physical contact in case of any fighting.

It was interesting to note that when we moved the cubs away from the kitchen, we needed to pick them up and weigh them before they went into the observation sett, so that we could monitor their growth. Although they had been living in the house with us, there had not, before now, been any real need to have any contact with them other than to feed them. They had lived in the kitchen with the freedom to explore further afield, and although used to these people walking around on long legs, who placed the food on the ground and made a lot of fuss about the mess afterwards, they basically were left alone and had each other for company. Only the ones that had been bottle-fed, Catkin, Acorn and Sorrell, would come up for attention. In picking the others up to transport them to their new home, they were so terrified of the experience that they defecated and became completely wild. One actually bit me quite badly through the nail. I have no qualms about rearing cubs in a domestic situation as long as physical contact is kept to a minimum.

After two weeks, we were able to put all six cubs and the sows together, and they all settled in very well. It was still necessary to keep the social group contained so that they could get used to their new home, but I still went down and let Bluebell out; she would come up to the house with me for the evening and then outside to forage before eventually returning home to the observation sett.

Bluebell seemed more placid than usual and there were occasions that she would climb on my lap and rest her head on my shoulder and just stay there. Something was not quite right. I wondered if she was upset at all the cubs being in the sett, although she actively sought them out when she returned to the sett.

Normally, our routine was that I would let her out and she would wander in the house and sniff around, and then go out foraging in the garden and homeground. As dusk fell, I would carry the food down to the enclosure and call to her. Always, before I had reached the pen, Bluebell had joined me and would pad along beside me. I noticed that she panted, but then we were still experiencing hot balmy evenings. She had such an appetite and was eating a lot of food; it was necessary for us to put a lot of food in the enclosures to make sure the adults would leave enough for the cubs.

It was at this time that a Belgian couple came and asked if they could get some photographs for a magazine. They wanted to do an article on badgers that come into people's homes. Johann and Santana came on several evenings and took many lovely photographs of Bluebell coming into the house. On one evening, much to my amazement, Bluebell came up to Johann as he sat on the stairs and bit him. In all the time that I had had her, even when she had cubs, Bluebell had never bitten anyone. It was almost as if she objected to anyone else being around, she just seemed to want to be with me.

I had no real symptoms to go by, but a gut feeling told me something was wrong, and so the next day I telephoned Stuart, the vet.

'It may be just a personality change,' he said, 'you say she hasn't lost weight. What makes you think something is wrong?'

'I don't know', I said, frowning. 'I just know something is not right. She keeps wanting to sit on my lap, she's not her usual self – and she's got a crush on custard creams!' I wailed.

'Sounds very serious,' he teased, but he had sensed my genuine concern. 'I think we'd better have her in and have a look. We'll need to take an X-ray, OK?'

It was a big step. Bluebell had never travelled in a car, or even been put in a carrying cage; as for getting her into the cage, I would probably have only one chance. There was no point in getting anyone to help me, as it would only make her more suspicious, so opening the door to the chambers, I waited for her to come out. As she always did, she sauntered out, backing against me to scent-mark me. Quickly I picked her up and placed her in the cage, fastening it before she had a chance to escape. I felt as if I had betrayed her. Placing the carrying cage with my precious cargo quickly into the car, I made my way to the vet's.

Stuart was waiting as I arrived.

'Hello, Bluebell,' he said as he took the cage from me, 'you're going to spend the day with me.' Looking up at me, he said, 'I'll give you a ring later. Don't worry, I'm sure she'll be all right.'

Clever little fox – unusually for foxes Kevin became so tame that
when released he just came straight back to the farm

Murray and Glade – who's chewing who?

Glade – the tiny baby badger who helped to console Pauline after the sadness of Bluebell's death

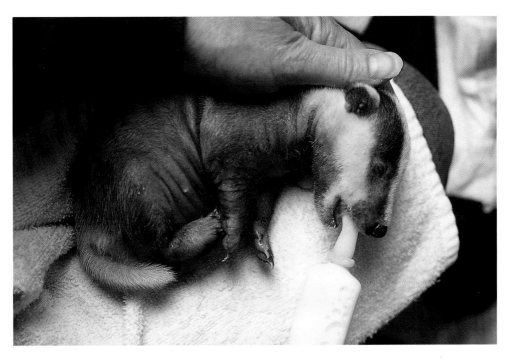

At 3 weeks, Glade tucks in to his bottle

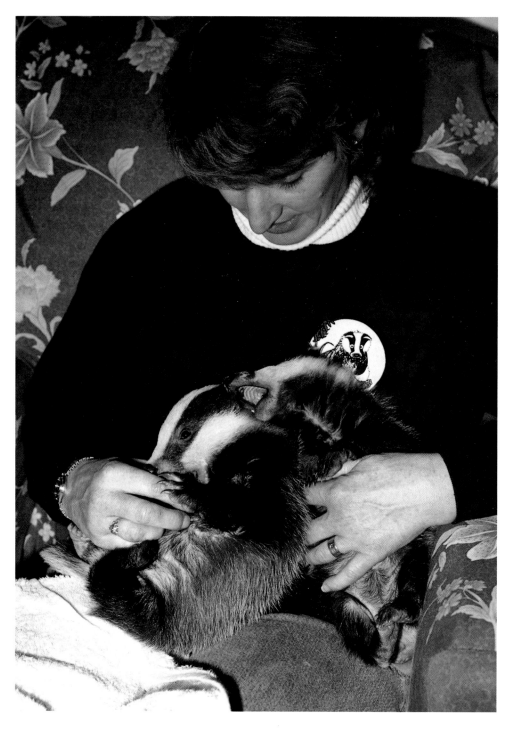

Sorrell and Acorn, two of the first cubs Bluebell helped to look after

Catkin, another of Bluebell's protégés, at 5 weeks old

Catkin investigates the dishwasher, while Sorrell is more interested in what's for dinner

Pauline and Bluebell

Bluebell pays a call at the front door, greeted by the author
and Barney

'Whatever you do,' I said to him, 'don't trust her, there's nothing as dangerous as a tame badger.'

I knew everything was going to be strange to her, and there was no knowing how she would cope with it. She was in capable hands, and part of me was relieved that, one way or the other, we would have an answer – but I half suspected that it was not going to be good news.

When Stuart finally contacted me later in the day, I could tell from his voice that I had been right.

'It's not good news, Pauline, I'm afraid,' Stuart gently explained. 'Bluebell has a serious chest infection and must be finding it very difficult to breathe. There is the problem that it could be TB and I have sent samples off – I don't think it is, but we are still faced with a serious situation. If you had left bringing her in for another three or four days, she would have been dead.'

Swallowing hard, I looked up at the ceiling, trying desperately not to cry, willing myself to keep control. I asked him what we were to do next.

'I think she will be happier at home with you, but put her in the care pen, so that you can keep an eye on her,' he explained. 'She'll need injections in the scruff of her neck every day for seven days, can you handle that?'

'Yes,' I said. 'Yes, I can manage that.'

'We will just have to wait for the results. If it is TB, it won't respond to the antibiotic, anyway. I'm sorry, Pauline, but it seems you were right, Bluebell is a very sick badger.'

I went immediately and brought her home. Inquisitively she explored the care pen, although she had been in one before when I had been decorating there one evening and she had come and joined me. I had put a large bedspread and blanket in there for her to lie on, and the heat lamp was switched on to give her warmth. Stupidly, I sat on the floor and as she had come to do, she sat on my lap. Burying my face into her body, I cried.

Later, I began to realize just how long I had been there – Derek must be wondering where on earth I was. Lifting her gently on to the blanket, I made my way out of the pen. Sure that she was going too, Bluebell got up and made her way to the door; I just managed to shut the door before she reached it.

Watching her through the viewing window, I saw her put her head on one side, listening to see if I had gone away. Lifting a paw she scratched at the door, and then both paws, digging at the door, cross that she had been left behind. It was not long before the effort was too much, and she ambled over to the blankets. Nosing the covers, she tossed the edge of her blanket over her head, and sank down in the bedding. She was completely and utterly fed up.

I went back to the pen before I went to bed, and felt happier at the sight of Bluebell now lying flat on her back, with all the warmth playing on her stomach. She looked very comfortable. I had done as much as I could for one day.

Peering in the next pen, I could see Mr Boar Badger, still with us. The hot weather is due to break, so the forecasters tell us; soon you will be able to go, I quietly told him. I hated seeing him in the pen, when he was well enough to be released, but there was really no point until we had had some rain.

Over the next few days, my spirits lifted. Bluebell seemed to be responding to the treatment and when the results came through two days later, she was given the all-clear. How lucky we were, I thought, that we had managed to catch it in time.

Stuart came out a week later, to give her a check-up. 'How's my favourite patient?' he said to her as he went in. 'She was brilliant, you know, when she was in the surgery – Colin (the other veterinary surgeon) just walked around with her in his arms. I told him Mrs Kidner says, you mustn't trust her, but she was fine.'

He listened to her chest and heart. She was, he declared, much better. 'Can she go back with the others?' I asked. 'I don't see why not.' He was as pleased as I was.

Later that afternoon, opening all the gates, we allowed Bluebell to run back to the observation sett and through into the chambers. All the cubs tumbled out to greet her and there was a great vocal greeting from all concerned. Acorn and Tansy turned to musk her, and Catkin, in her excitement, managed to climb on her back and land on Bluebell's head. Climbing into the largest chamber, Bluebell flopped down in the straw, happy to be home. All six cubs piled in with her, preening through her hair, fighting each other and eventually settling down. With Bluebell and the cubs settled in one chamber and Clover and Snowdrop together in another, it was a lovely sight.

The rains came at last; a solid week of almost continuous rain turned the scorched brown lawns to evergreen carpets. Drainpipes dripped as torrents of water ran down our old brick courtyard. Everything glistened and there was a smell of freshness in the warm summer air. 'Time for you', I said to Mr Boar Badger, 'to go home!'

People have said to me before, 'how do you manage to pick up a big boar badger when you are called out to them?' That is usually the easy part, because they are mostly injured and weak. The fun starts when they are healthy and fit, and have maybe gained quite a bit of weight, and you are trying to get them back in the box to take them home!

With the cage on its side, I gently cajoled the badger into the corner. I can usually, by pushing against his feet, get a badger into the cage, but because it is top-opening, it is then a question of quickly flicking the cage over and shutting the lid before he has time to jump out again. Sounds easy, doesn't it?

Actually Mr Boar Badger was quite helpful and he was contained first try. Loading him into the van, Mandy and I were soon back at the farm where he had come from a couple of months before. Though he was quiet in the car, he recognized his surroundings as we arrived and, as soon as we placed the cage on the ground, he was very keen to get out! Carefully opening the lid of the cage, Mandy quickly stepped back, as without any hesitation the badger jumped out of the cage and ran immediately to where a badger path passed through a hedgerow. I was so pleased he was back out in the open; I just hoped he would manage to survive.

The cubs enjoyed the rain in the enclosure; worms had come to the surface and instinctively the badgers began to forage. Acorn loved the pond and would regularly walk straight in and snorkel around the perimeter for beetles and bugs. He would even sit in the middle and preen – a show-off if ever there was one! My three bottle-fed cubs would still come up to me, but the others were much more wary and I could only really monitor them by watching them in the glass chambers.

I was continuing to take Bluebell out in the evenings. Despite being better she still spent a lot of the time in the house with me and after a period of time became aggressive towards the boys, Simon and Daniel, who were home on summer holidays from university. It was so unlike her. It was the same as before – she just wanted to be with me and wanted no one else around.

All through her life, I have at times had her out with visitors and she has been super with children. We have had as many as thirty in the observation area, and she has come out and scent-marked people's feet and allowed them to stroke her. On this occasion,

I had her out as a small group from a local badger group were visiting. As we talked, a couple with two young children came in. One child had some sweets and Bluebell, smelling them, went forward to get them. The other child, scared by her approach, became hysterical and jumped up on the seats. At any other time, if Blue has been scared she would scuttle back into the chambers, but this time she went after the child and she meant it. Grabbing her by whatever I could get hold of, I pulled her away from the seats and threw her into the back section of the sett. Even then she came back, charging as I shut the door. Apart from being frightened, the child was all right. The parents were very understanding and, in fact, thought that it was the pitch of the child's scream that set Bluebell off. I mentally vowed that I would never have Bluebell out with other people again.

I was back to ringing Stuart again. 'I'm sorry, but I'm sure there is something wrong again. Bluebell looks fine, her coat shines, she is heavy but she has turned aggressive.' Stuart quickly agreed to see her again. It was only a month since she had been given the all-clear but as I had been right before, he could not ignore my instincts.

Once again I had to betray her trust and trick her into a cage, this time with even more apprehension than before. She was not so easy to carry either, as she now weighed over 40 pounds.

'Well,' said Stuart when he rang later with the results, 'you were right about her being aggressive. I've just finished sewing my finger up!'

As Stuart was anaesthetizing her, Bluebell had tried to give him a 'friendly nip', as he described it, and so he had thought that he had better give a higher dose. He was about to administer the injection to her, when with lightning reactions she had bitten him through the joint of his finger. He admitted to me later that he had had some doubts as to whether she was going to let go.

'Pauline, she is very ill again. Her lungs are as bad as they were before and we obviously have a serious underlying problem here. The only way forward is to inject her with higher levels of antibiotics over a longer period.' We had already found that to try and get her to take anything orally was practically impossible, for the badger's sense of smell is so acute that they just won't eat anything that has been doctored.

'Now the problem is', said Stuart, 'that she is very dangerous and I am not happy about expecting you to do this.

Bluebell is a very big badger and could do a lot of damage.'

'Well,' I said, knowing full well what he was saying, 'if anyone can inject her, it will be me, and if it becomes too dangerous then we shall have to consider the option of euthanasia.'

'You can come and get her when you want; I'll put up all the drugs and the instructions, but whatever you do, Pauline, be careful,' Stuart warned me.

'Oh, Blue,' I said to her, as I put her back in the care pen. 'What am I going to do with you?' She padded up to me and placed her head on my knees, but to my shame I must admit the trust had gone, and whilst I still fondled her head, my wits were about me and I was ready to move.

I had to inject her every day for three weeks, and the first day was the worst. She was quivering in one corner because she could sense I was about to do something, and I was quivering in the other corner wondering if she was going to go for me. Before, I had given her some custard creams to eat while I injected her, but that confidence had gone, and I covered her with a blanket and injected her as I turned the blanket back. As I moved the blanket away, just for a second, she thought about charging at me but then she relaxed and just settled on her bedding. Bluebell could not help it, it was part of her condition. She could not understand why suddenly it was so difficult to breathe and everything was such an effort.

Slowly, once again we built up our trust with each other. Bluebell got used to the routine of the injections and cleaning out and I allowed no one else in with her. She again responded to the treatment although her appetite was voracious. Stuart advised that we gave her as much as she could eat, and there were times when she was clearing a large icecream container of food each day. Gradually her health seemed to recover. Stuart explained that with lung infections, sometimes as much damage is done by the healing process of scarring the soft tissues of the lung as by the disease itself; it was bound to take time.

Maybe because Bluebell was missing from the sett, Catkin found a way of escaping from the enclosure and was frequently found dancing on the lawn in the evening. If no one noticed her, she would be sat outside the observation sett door the next morning, waiting for someone to let her back in – she was a real scamp!

After three weeks of injections and a final X-ray, my hopes were raised and again Bluebell returned to the sett. With Bluebell as the staying power, we decided to open the gates and allow the badgers their freedom.

All the hard work and the heartache was behind me now in the thrill of sitting on the lawn, with Catkin tumbling over my legs and Bluebell playing once again as she charged around us. In the damp September evenings, I could just make out the silhouettes of the other badgers, foraging against the hedge but no longer trusting me to come as close as Catkin and Bluebell did. But they had obviously made the farm their home.

The sett that Bluebell had dug in the front garden was opened up even further and the social group shared their time between the observation sett and the garden sett. Bedding trails were dragged from the nearby barn into the garden and badger paths began to appear around the farm as they built up their territories. Once again, I could walk around the farm with Bluebell as company and now Catkin too! How lucky I was.

A call from just down the road sent Derek and me to a local farm where an injured badger was reported. It was in the barn, under some wooden planks. As there were doors to the barn, we were able to contain it and capture was not too difficult as the badger was weak from his injuries. Taking him back to the farm, we put him into a care pen and Derek went to ring the vet, to let them know we would be coming through with a badger. Looking through the window, I could see that the territorial bite at the back of his rump was seething with maggots. Dirty and tired, the badger moved towards the lamp and slowly turned his face to me. It was the first time I had really looked at his face. As soon as I looked, I knew him. The scar down the side of his nose and the pink blotches told me Mr Boar Badger was back. All that time in getting him better, keeping him while there was a drought, clever old me – all I had done was to put him back to suffer all over again the pain and the anguish of being the unwanted social group member. I vowed that never again would I try to heal an old badger, no matter what attention had been given to its wounds. Who am I to think that I can change nature? We took the badger into the vet, but we didn't bring him back. I'm just sorry for the suffering I caused him.

I had been out for the evening a few days later and, arriving back late, I saw a black bag dumped by the back door. People do sometimes bring us dead badgers that they find on the road, so I half suspected that it was going to be a dead animal. As I undid the bag, I could tell it had only just died as the body was still warm, and indeed it was a badger. When I pulled back the side of the bag, a beautifully marked head of a young juvenile badger could be seen. I have now, as part of my job, seen many dead badgers and it always fills me with sadness, but this one was a face that I knew, one that I had loved. It was my Catkin. She had been knocked down just outside our farm. How short her little life had been.

There were so many memories of her as a cub – she was always the pickle. Catkin had got over her bowel problem when she had started to eat solids, and from a dreadful bald scruffy cub, she had grown into a fine juvenile badger. Cupping her tiny head in my hand, I said goodbye to a little soul who had given me so much joy.

I was cross that I had released them from our centre, as some of the release sites used are miles away from roads. If she had been sent to one of those she could still be alive, I blamed myself. In reality, there had not been enough release sites anyway. Just in that one season we had dealt with seventeen badger cubs, eleven of which survived; our 'kitchen crew' were six of them and a further five were included in social groups at the RSPCA. Having been reared on the farm, Catkin had grown up knowing her territory, which made it more likely that she would stay; and we had never had a badger run over on our road before. Why now, why her, why?

There are always times when life seems to kick you in the teeth, and I do try to think on the positive side. At least things can not get worse, I thought; I was wrong.

It all happened within the same week. Catkin died on the Saturday, and the incident at Wembdon where the badgers were buried under tons of soil was carried out on the Monday. The following Thursday, I was giving a talk to a church group at Cannington. While I was away in the afternoon, Bluebell suddenly began to feel very ill and dragged herself out of the observation sett, through the field and was found by a member of staff outside the casualty pens. She knew she needed help. My son, Simon, immediately took her to the vet's. On my way home, I passed the vet and thought about calling in for some dog food. We were on the last bag, but it wasn't urgent so I hesitated as to whether or not to go in as there was a lot of traffic on the road. Eventually I decided to go in. As soon as I went in the receptionist said, 'Have you come to see how Bluebell is?' and I knew straightaway that something was very wrong. The receptionist took me through to the back room where Bluebell was still in her cage but breathing very deeply. She roused as I went in, and I knelt by her cage.

Matter of factly, Mark went through the reasons for her collapse. In a way I was listening, but I knew as soon as I saw her that she was slipping away. Bluebell made a load groan, arched her back and relaxed. Her body was still. Lifting her out on to the table it was quite clear that she was dead. In those few minutes that I had been there, almost as if she had been waiting for me, she had finally died – she had always trusted me.

Just at that point Stuart rushed in, having only just heard that she had been admitted. 'Oh, Blue,' he said, caressing her head.

Leaving her for a post mortem, I said, 'I'll come back for her', and I left quickly before I had to say any more.

The post mortem results basically showed that her lungs were in such a bad condition that there was no way she would ever have recovered. There had been so many people who had constantly kept in contact while Bluebell was ill that it was easier to send a press release to badger groups telling them she had died. It was also broadcast on television and radio – so many people had known her. The press release was as follows.

BLUEBELL

It was late February 1989 when Bluebell arrived at New Road Farm along with her siblings, Willow and Primrose. They had been orphaned when their mother was accidentally killed by a local building contractor laying drainage pipes. On finding the three cubs still suckling their dead mother, one of the workmen remembered the Farm and brought them into Pauline Kidner's care.

When she arrived at the farm, Bluebell was about five weeks old and just eight inches long. She had a velvet coat and her eyes were only just beginning to open, but she already had her long claws and distinctive striped face.

It was with Bluebell, Primrose and Willow, that Pauline first came to the public's attention with pictures of them walking in the fields together: and it was this publicity that brought Simon King to the farm so he could film the infant Bluebell.

Although the other badgers eventually left the farm, Bluebell continued to return each night – she had decided that the farm was to be her home. She carefully dug (although never used) a spare sett in the flower beds at the front of the house and when the door was open, often came in to see Pauline and scrounge biscuits.

On 28th February 1992, Bluebell gave birth to two cubs and during that year raised not just her own but three other orphaned cubs that were brought to us. She continued to teach young cubs how to become real badgers each year and, when it was decided to establish a separate name for the support group to finance the wildlife work at the Farm, the name 'Bluebell Sett' was chosen.

In late summer 1994, Bluebell became ill and had to be separated from the other badgers in the observation sett. She developed a lung infection with pleuritis and inflammation of the chest cavity. This was successfully treated for a time but then her condition deteriorated again as her white blood cell count plummeted. Apparently past this crisis and reunited with the other badgers, she once again fell ill with broncho-pneumonia.

Bluebell badger died on 8th September 1994.

Work will continue in her name at Pauline's Badger and Wildlife Rescue Centre at Secret World where Bluebell will be fondly remembered by all.

Bluebell was buried at the front of the farm in a special flower bed that was created just for her. A large stone bearing her name marks the place and the floodlight at night illuminates the place in memory of her. It is there that I visit nearly every night and the first thing I see every time I come home.

No one, unless they too have experienced such a deep relationship with a wild creature, can understand the tremendous loss that I feel. No longer does that black and white face follow me in my nightly walks, no more romps on the lawn. It was my privilege to have shared her life – I shall never forget her. She was my Blue.

I had never felt so washed up, exhausted from the long hours, worn out by the feeling of failure. I don't think anyone involved with caring for wild animals doesn't have a time when they question what they are doing, the times of utter uselessness and senseless waste. So often people say, how lucky we are to do the work that we do – and we are, but oh, the pain, the sense of loss when things go wrong.

For years we had struggled with the bank on our backs, trying to finance the work that we do, and always, at the back of my mind, had been the terrifying thought that if we lost the farm, what would happen to Bluebell?

I was lucky in marriage: whatever life could throw at us, Derek and I could manage somehow. But now the responsibility had gone, and I felt weary, even empty; I felt as if I could just walk away from it all – it hurt too much.

9

After Bluebell

Without Bluebell in the observation sett, the other badgers began to use the outside sett more regularly. I decided it would be better to build an artificial sett for the social group and exclude them from the observation sett and enclosure, so that these could be used for badgers that have to be kept in captivity for a period of time. We built the sett just outside the enclosure with help from a local firm who lent us a digger, and with the aid of volunteers the new 'home' was created in a day – and the badgers moved in that very night!

I think, in a way, I was preparing for the problem that might have arisen if we had had to sell the farm. With an artificial and a natural sett, the badgers had plenty of room even if the observation sett had to be closed down. The only thing that really worried me now were the girls that worked for us, who dearly love the animals they are involved with – what would happen to them if everything had to go?

October passed by and we were already in November, yet still my enthusiasm was low. I had been out all day having spent most of the afternoon giving a slide talk to a group of retired people. It had gone well and I had enjoyed showing the many lovely slides of all the different animals that have come to us, and telling the funny stories of things that happen on the farm.

One story I had retold was of how our long-suffering local people have to put up with my unusual requests. We were hand-rearing two very young grey squirrels one spring and they were doing well, but the female squirrel tended to comfort-suck the penis of her young brother. Maybe in a different situation this may have given the unfortunate little boy squirrel quite a lot of pleasure, but at such an early age, and with his penis becoming rather sore and bright pink, it was a situation that needed to be resolved.

It is at times like these that my inspiration works wonders and I was soon found telephoning our local pharmacist for advice. My request caused a lot of amusement, and to be honest the poor man was stumped at my question and had to look the answer up – advise me he did however, and the problem was solved after a short journey to the chemist. The little boy squirrel, with his penis smothered in vaseline and dipped in bitter aloes, no longer had the undesired interest of his sister!

It is a lovely feeling when other people can enjoy hearing about the work that we do and so often this will promote further interest in the wildlife around us.

By the time I arrived home, the night was already drawing in. Turning in to the farm, I passed Bluebell's flower bed and noticed that already the bulbs were shooting through. When spring arrived there would be a show of blue flowers bursting into bloom in her memory.

I drove slowly through the gravel yard noticing the flocks of starlings circling our garden, vast numbers coming in from different directions noisily greeting each other. We have been a winter roost for many years. I find it fascinating to see them congregating in groups that make the sky almost black by the sheer numbers of them. Weaving and twisting, the throng of birds flew down to the conifer trees, to settle only momentarily before taking off again to swoop down towards the ponds before returning to the trees.

They may be among the commonest of birds, but looked at closely, their colouring is beautiful especially during the breeding season when the white tips to their feathers contrast with their iridescent blue-black colouring. Happy to eat almost anything, they adapt to either town or country conditions, and it is due to this adaptability that their numbers have increased. Goodness knows how many we have roosting here but their numbers can be over a million in a single roost as they swarm like bees, congregating at a regular site with each bird using a particular tree, even a particular branch, every night. At dawn they leave in the same way as they came, groups flying off at regular intervals, returning yet again the following evening.

Soon the air would be full of song as spring arrived and they sang for a mate. It is easy to become confused by the song of a starling as they can be great mimics, often copying birds such as curlews, coots and tawny owls – even the human voice! Untidy nests will appear in the eaves of the house or the many holes in our old and twisting apple trees in the orchard. Broken pale blue eggshells will be seen scattered around, proof that the young have hatched, the eggshells being discarded by the parent birds to keep the nests clean; and the busy time of constantly feeding the young, the new generation, will start again.

I was aware of how life goes on, each season followed by the next. How lucky I was that I could see this spectacle each evening, accepting it almost without recognizing how synchronized things in nature are, the routine of wildlife about us that we are largely unaware of.

The girls, having finished their day, gathered up their coats and bags and, waving goodbye, crossed the floodlit yard, now silent as darkness fell. Derek was off to cricket practice that evening and soon I was alone in the house with the sound of the rain beating against the window.

Sitting drinking my coffee in the big armchair in the kitchen, I glanced around the room. All the dogs were sleeping after a full day charging around the farm. Sam, our little schnauzer, lay by the fire, her back legs sprawled out behind her as the heat sent her to sleep. Barney, as usual, had commandeered the other armchair, the masses of brown curly hair making it impossible to see if his eyes were closed or open; but the twitching of his legs showed that he was sound asleep, dreaming of chasing those rabbits that he never manages to catch. Murray, my 'little puppy', was stretched out next to Sam by the fire. His huge frame takes up so much room that to walk round the kitchen these days is more a question of finding a part of the kitchen floor that isn't already covered! The

RSPCA had come out the previous week to do a home check since we had now had him for six months, and they were visiting to see that he was still all right. On looking at the breed entered on his chart, I noticed that he was down as an Alsatian X Doberman.

Poor Derek – he puts up with so much. Murray's size matches his enthusiasm and as Derek is usually the first one up in the morning, it is he who faces the welcome as Murray thunders down the hall as soon as he hears someone about. One morning, Derek had pulled on his dressing gown and gone to switch on the kettle in the kitchen when I heard the pounding footsteps making their way towards Derek in the hall. The unavoidable impact was greeted with sworn oath and hurried human and dog footsteps raced back to the bedroom door. Derek, having won the competition, slammed the door in Murray's face, managing to exclude him from the bedroom. 'Your dog,' came the accusing comment (funny how it's always mine when it has done something wrong), 'your dog,' repeated Derek, making sure that I was awake to hear this complaint, 'has come charging down the hall and reached me just as my dressing gown fell open and he has severely scratched my scrotum!' The tone of the voice was such that I was indeed wide awake and doing my best to administer sympathy without laughing. I kept my face under the covers.

Pulling on his clothes for safety's sake, Derek attempted to journey to the kitchen for a second time, prepared for the onslaught. But I still got my coffee in bed, so I must have been forgiven.

Now seeing Murray and all the dogs asleep, everything seemed quiet. I glanced around my kitchen, my haven – could I really give up this?

Loath to leave the warmth of the kitchen, I made the effort, as I still had to feed the badgers that were in the observation sett. We had two badgers in for the winter, boars that were too late for the release groups the previous summer; they would be released the next year together with any cubs that had been raised.

As soon as I moved, everyone was up and we made our way downstairs. Pulling on my heavy denim jacket to ward off the cold wind, I collected the food for the badgers. The dogs stayed up in the play area and, using my torch, I made my way to the bottom part of the farm.

Little owls screeched from the homeground as the beam from my torch lit my way down by the poultry pens. As usual I shone my torch up into the large conker tree as I passed it, methodically counting the peafowl and guinea-fowl roosted in the large bare arms of the tree, seemingly oblivious to the cold wind blowing across our flat countryside. The long trains of the peafowl billowed in the wind and I wondered how they managed to keep their balance at times.

Briefly I saw a black and white face dart over to the hay barn. It still thrills me to see my badgers about the farm. Switching off the torch, I leant against the rail of the fence and watched. It was a full moon so I could see quite well without the torch. First I heard the shuffling, and then slowly a large grey rump heaved backwards in an ungainly movement towards the artificial sett. It was Acorn. With a bundle of dry yellow straw tucked under his chin, he was completely absorbed in the matter in hand, which was a bedding trail from the hay barn to the artificial sett. Dragging his important load, he backed across the concrete, occasionally rolling the bedding back up into a ball with his paw, keeping it tidy so as not to lose too many bits and pieces. With a precise sense of direction, he backed up to the tunnel entrance of the sett, and waddling side to side to make his backside fit, he eventually disappeared from view. What a lucky badger, not just a free home but soft furnishings as well!

I continued down to the observation sett, and placed the food in the enclosure for the two badgers, throwing it around in the pen to encourage them to forage for it. It will be nice, I thought, when they too can have their freedom.

The sheep paddock, which we have to go through to get to the enclosure, was very muddy with all the rain we had been having. As I slowly picked my way I glimpsed the barn owls in Simon King's aviary hovering over the tray where their food had been put. The pen is really large, allowing them to fly and hover as they would do in the wild. Having been captive-bred they must think it ideal to have such a large enclosure. These were the birds used for the film 'Tyto the Barn Owl' which Simon made in 1994. Now they will spend the rest of their lives with us and it is pleasing to know they have such good living conditions.

On my way up, I checked the casualty pens. The first one housed the hedgehogs that we were overwintering as they were underweight. Most of them were out, making the most of the food supplied for them which they would find so hard to forage for during the winter.

Sage, our barn owl, called out a greeting to me, on hearing my voice. He stays in the casualty pens during the winter as he is quite old now, and enjoys the comfort of an infra-red lamp on the cold nights. Nosy as usual, he flew to the netting to get his head scratched.

One pen contains a badger with a broken leg. Going into the pen quietly, I turned her over on to her opposite side to stop her getting stiff. As I quietly talk to her, she watches me. Now that she is used to our routine she is not so nervous, although I still treat her with respect! She is going to take a long time to get better, if we are lucky enough to win the day, as it was a bad break.

The last pen I checked housed a boar badger that was in with territorial wounds. There was no need to open his pen, as I could see him quite clearly through the viewing window, stretched out on his blanket under the infra-red lamp. Linda Groves, who is a member of the Bluebell Sett Committee, had come with me to pick him up. He had been found in a garden in the middle of Weston-super-Mare; the householder had been quite irate at this badger that had entered through a cat flap into a garden all landscaped with raised flower beds, and who had then proceeded to find a way out by digging not in just one but in practically every flower bed, all to no avail.

It was a very built-up area, and I tend to think that a badger out during the day in the wrong place usually means trouble. So we decided to put him into a carrying box and take him back to the centre to give him a check-over. It was the first time that Linda had been out to collect a badger and she was keen to watch how it was done. The badger was curled in a ball behind some shrubs and looked very small. Covering him with a blanket, I felt for the scruff of his neck and his rump and lifted him up. The more I lifted, the bigger the badger became! He had dug himself down and in fact we had just been looking at the top of him, so the small juvenile turned out to be a large male. He made no attempt to fight and I placed him in the cage. Linda was very impressed. 'You make it look so easy!' she remarked.

'Believe you me,' I retorted, 'it was; they are not usually as helpful as that.'

Urbie, as Linda called him seeing as he was found in an urban area, was soon on his way to our centre. Upon examination, he did not appear to have any injuries, so we discussed putting him back near to where he came from. However, he did not eat the first night so I decided to hold on to him. The next night was a Friday, and even if we had wanted to put him back, we would have been too busy to have done so then, or on Saturday. By the Sunday, I could smell that he had some trouble around his ear and he was taken into the vet's. He was found to have an abscess inside the ear which was obviously causing him pain. He was put on antibiotics, and the following day anaesthetized and given a clean-up. A course of injections helped him fight the infection and then he was to be kept for a further five days to recover fully.

Looking at him that night, I noticed from his record sheet that it would soon be time for him to be returned to his home. We sometimes question whether it is right to let them go back into developed areas, but then they have survived in that kind of territory so who are we to doubt the suitability of it? I made a mental note to ring Linda about releasing him.

Quietly shutting the gate to the care pens, I thought of all the work that we do. A few months ago, Blue would have been waiting on the other side of the gate – having sensed that I was about, she would have sought me out. Maybe it is hard work, and somewhere we have got to find money for our new enclosures, but for the sake of the animals that come to us and to make people aware of the need to care about our countryside, I was determined to carry on.

We have so much support from people in many different ways. The girls that work for us, some on training schemes and not earning very much, work very hard and genuinely care for all our animals. They are greatly appreciated, as are our volunteers, many of whom have been transformed from just liking animals to having to cope with the depths of blood, muck and thunder – and even cutting up dead chicks! They all have their stories to tell.

Becky came to us straight from school, bright and bubbly. She was keen to learn and would follow instructions to the letter. When dealing with animals, you have to come to terms with the fact that there will always be live animals and dead animals. If an unfortunate casualty dies then we try to dispose of the body as cleanly as possible; our Rayburn is usually going most of the time and we will incinerate bodies on there as long as they will fit! On one occasion, Becky was working with Mandy and sadly one of the hedgehogs had died during the night in the sickroom. Entering on to its card that it had died, Mandy wrapped the dead hedgehog up in newspaper and told Becky to put it on the Rayburn in the kitchen, which she dutifully did.

Returning to the house from working in the office, I came into the kitchen and sensed an unusual smell. To be quite honest, I thought someone had been out to get some fish and chips because it was the smell that you usually get when you place the fish and chips in the oven to warm up again before serving, having left them still in the newspaper.

Glancing over at the Rayburn, I was surprised to see a package placed on the top of the hotplate, which was starting to smoke quite strongly. Picking up the offending parcel with a pair of tongs, I realized what had happened. Mandy meant for Becky to open the fire door of the Rayburn and place the body inside, whereas Becky had placed the newspaper parcel on the hotplate where it was simmering gently! It was a long time before she was allowed to forget her attempt at cooking a hedgehog, rather than incinerating it!

The episode with Martine was to be my embarrassment. Martine, who joined us as a volunteer, is a very attractive young lady, with a perfect figure and make-up to match. Long wavy golden locks of hair cascade from a pony tail on top of her head, crowning the kind of looks that turn men's heads. Wherever Martine goes, there is usually a man carrying a bucket for her. However, she is brilliant with the animals and has a lovely way with them.

When she first arrived, Derek was busy talking to Simon King and some of his work-force who were here filming. 'Who's that?' one of the men remarked.

'Our new volunteer,' said Derek, smiling at their interest.

'Well, if she needs any help . . .' came the reply.

That evening I showed her how to feed a baby pipistrelle bat with a dropper; once fed, I slipped it into a small pouch which I usually wear around my neck. Bats live in groups roosting very close together, and we have found that baby bats are happier next to a heartbeat rather than leaving them solitary in a box.

'You're on duty,' I said to Martine, offering her the bat in the bag to wear while she was at the farm.

'Right,' she said, slipping the cord over her neck and popping the bag inside her jumper for warmth, in the same way as I do. I left her to feed a baby rabbit while I brought the washing in. Taking all the towels into the sickroom, I started to fold them, ready to put them away.

'Is the baby rabbit feeding OK?' I asked.

'Yes,' said Martine, 'and – Oh! . . .' She stopped what she was saying, and felt the front of her t-shirt. 'Oh,' she said, 'I think the baby bat has escaped.'

I walked towards her. Deftly, she lifted her t-shirt, displaying a very pretty lace black bra, very nicely filled. God, I thought, she's got everything – looks *and* boobs. 'Can you find it?' she said, very perturbed for the baby bat's safety.

Let me tell you, it is very difficult to find a very small black bat hidden in an intricately laced bra, and I took so long that I was beginning to think she might doubt my intentions. Both she and I were relieved when I eventually located it and bat and t-shirt were back in place.

I went off to finish my chores and passed Derek still talking to the lads. 'What are you smiling about?' Derek asked, and I told them of the incident. 'Cor!', said one of them. 'We could have helped, couldn't we, lads?' Needless to say, they all agreed!

All of our staff work well as a team, but wildlife care extends much further than that; for although we care for injured animals, if it were not for the people who take the time either to report injured animals or even bring them in, then we would not be able to relieve their suffering. Even if we are then able to get the animals better, some are unable to return to where they came from and we are dependent on other people to find suitable sites for their eventual release. Territories have to be found that are suitable, that can support them for food and yet are vacant, and this all takes time. For every badger cub that is taken into care, you are talking about approximately fifteen months' work in order to get them back into the wild.

A series of projects must be carried out by different people in order to make this release successful. Badgers are territorial animals and so you cannot release them into areas already belonging to another social group of badgers, because they will fight and even kill each other. During the winter months, when all the natural vegetation has died down, someone has to go out and survey the countryside to find a territory where there are no badgers at all but that can still support the foraging of a social group. These territories are particularly difficult to find in the south-west of England, which already contains 25 per cent of the badger population found in the British Isles. This is why, very often, social groups go for release in other counties such as Essex and Suffolk. Once these territories are found, they are recorded with people such as Colin Seddon at the RSPCA, who are responsible for the rehabilitation of the groups of hand-reared badgers ready to be released the following autumn.

Most of the orphaned and injured badger cubs start to come in from March onwards, as this is the time that they start to emerge and forage for themselves. The badger cubs are reared and weaned by different people throughout the country, but it is important that, whenever possible, a badger cub is not reared on its own. This is necessary for any animal or bird, because if it is reared in a solitary situation with no other member of its own species to interact with, the animal will become imprinted, relating only to the person rearing it, therefore thinking it is a human being. Once an animal is imprinted, identifying itself only with human beings, it can never be returned to the wild. Badgers in particular are very gregarious, being family creatures, and must have the interaction of play and bonding.

As soon as possible, once weaned, the badger cubs are placed into social groups of up to ten animals, preferably as balanced as possible into equal numbers of male and female. They are put into large enclosures to reduce human contact, allowing them to revert to being wild, and offering the chance to start foraging naturally for their food.

When they are approximately six months of age, the social group is moved to their new territory. This is usually from July onwards. To start with they are enclosed by electric fencing, and a temporary home made of straw bales is used for accommodation until they have dug alternative setts themselves; this they do quite quickly, especially if there are already some unused rabbit holes.

Once they have been introduced to their new territories, some-one is responsible for feeding and checking on them every day for approximately six months. By this time they will have dug escape tunnels out from their enclosed areas, but it has been found that while creating their own escape routes they continue to go in and out, keeping to the territory allocated to them. The electric fence is then removed. They would now be going into the spring of the following year so the feeding is slowly reduced and they are then left to fend for themselves.

From the time of finding the territory, to the time of no support at all, is around fifteen months. Every person involved at each stage of the project is important to the success of the badgers' release. At the time of writing it is now four years since we started this scheme, and it is felt that this type of release is successful because cub groups released at the very beginning of the scheme have since stayed in their territories and bred their own cubs.

Different methods of release are used by other badger groups. Certainly the idea of temporary setts made of straw would be no use in Yorkshire where the persecution of badgers is so high (80 per cent of all their setts being dug), because the straw bales would be like an advert to the diggers to come and get them. Unfortunately, in these areas, it is necessary for very dedicated people to reinforce setts created in their county with wire mesh and concrete – what a sad reflection on the human race, that people can still be found today who delight in cruelty. All badgers that are moved from one county to another should be tested for TB and indeed, in Wales, a licence is required to transport them as well.

Foxes are another animal it is difficult to find release sites for, and recent research has questioned how successful they are in adapting to the wild after being reared in captivity. However, I think it is dangerous to come to conclusions based on limited research that has, after all, only been done in one area of the country, at one particular time of year, tracking foxes by radio collar. The more we learn from research the better, but it is important to keep an open mind to the fact that each situation is individual and must be treated as so.

I have had support from people I have never met. A farming magazine had an article on our centre and my interest in badgers, and this was followed a few weeks later by an article written by a farmer saying how many lambs he had lost through badgers killing them and raising the old issue of the relationship between badgers and cows in connection with TB. I say the 'old issue' because it is a sad fact that, for nearly 20 years, the government has been unable to prove beyond doubt that there is a link between badgers and TB in cows; and yet they have continued to cull badgers at a cost of £1.2 million a year because they have to 'be seen to be doing something', despite the fact that the testing method and the test itself are completely flawed.

However, there was a farmer in Scotland, Mr Drew, who read our article and was concerned that I would be upset by the article blaming the badgers for damage and TB. He took the time to telephone me, to assure me that there were many farmers who thought the culling was wrong. He had a very thick Scottish accent, and I sometimes found it hard to follow him, but the conversation was a delight.

'I did nae want ye to be upset,' he said. 'I hope ye dinna mind me saying, but you de have the trouble with the moisture down there and 'tis the cattle. My friend, Jimmy McCavish, moved down to Somerset, but he did ne keep the cattle on the farm, he bought clean cattle from Scotland, and he had ne'er had any trouble in all the time he's been there. 'Tis no need to kill the badger. Even I know that the only way that TB can be passed on is by the blood, the saliva or the urine.' His sing-song voice was getting louder as he got to his point.

'Now,' said Mr Drew, 'badgers and cows, they dinna eat each other, so it can ne be the blood. And a badger dinna kiss a coo – the only way it could be passed on is by urine and we electric fence away the dung pits and we have nae trouble at all.'

I thanked him for ringing me – 'If ye ever need a farmer to be quoted as liking badgers, you can contact me,' he said. Mr Drew – you have been quoted! Surely one day the government will see sense and the killing will stop. How can killing 5,000 animals every year be right when it has not improved the situation?

When we learnt that we had won the Animal Country Award

it really boosted our commitment, and the money meant that our enclosures could soon be under way. Care for the Wild, a charity that does so much to help wildlife care all over the world, also had offered some money towards our pens – suddenly what had seemed impossible was beginning to take shape.

The Bluebell Sett Wildlife Group goes from strength to strength with committee members working very hard to support us, and they become involved in everything we do. Events are organized to raise money and every amount of effort put in by dedicated people, be it large or small, helps us continue. One fantastic effort was by a Bluebell Sett member called Hazel Woods; her sheer determination helped her train and be successful in running the London Marathon for us, raising over £1,200 in sponsorship. It is so nice when I can involve these hard-working people in the enjoyment of what we do.

Linda did her first release when she offered to take Urbie home. He had recovered from his infection and it was important for him to return to his territory, even if it was a very built-up area. At the back of the garden where he was found was a large playing field and we decided to release him there as it was obviously a foraging area, with the short grass supplying the worms that form the badger's staple diet.

Linda drove over to the farm at midnight and we crated Urbie up for his journey home. When I had explained to her what to do, Linda went off, excited at the chance to let the badger go. Waving her goodbye, I wished her and Urbie luck under my breath as the car swung into the road and the tail lights disappeared towards the nearby bridge.

Linda arrived at the playing field half an hour later and, although Urbie was quiet on the journey, as soon as Linda lifted the cage into the playing field, he scratched frantically at the wire. He knew he was home. Leaving him just for a few minutes to adjust to his surroundings, Linda then opened the door and he ran like a bullet towards the other side of the field. Then came the magic. Suddenly she saw him running along the side of the fence, but now he was not on his own but had been joined by another badger. Momentarily they frolicked, whickering greetings to each other, excited at seeing each other. 'I'm home, I'm home,' he seemed to be saying; and then suddenly they were gone and the playing field went back to being the quiet empty place that it had been before.

'It was fantastic,' she exclaimed as she told me on the telephone the next day. 'I can understand why you love doing it so much.'

The joys and the sorrows of looking after animals.

Me? I couldn't give it up, could I? Spring has come round again and already I am sitting in my chair in the kitchen with a tiny baby badger curled up in my arms – a little boy who as yet has not opened his eyes and is probably only three weeks old. His tiny black and white head snuggles into me as he squirms his silver-grey body into the fold of my arm for the comfort of company.

I have called him Glade. In the forest, when an old tree falls a space is created and flower seeds that may have been dormant for over a hundred years will spring to life. Slowly, new trees will seed themselves and begin to grow and a new young habitat will be created from the space made by the fallen tree. He will be the new start for the year, in which there will be much to be done, I am sure.

No, there will never be another Bluebell, that time has gone. But I have many very happy memories and, I hope, many more to come.

Useful Addresses

Royal Society for the Prevention of Cruelty to Animals Wildlife Centres:

RSPCA Wildlife Field Unit,
West Hatch,
Taunton,
Somerset TA3 5RT

Tel: 01823 480156

RSPCA Norfolk Wildlife Hospital,
East Winch,
Norfolk PE32 1NR

Tel: 01553 840045

British Wildlife Rehabilitation Council, for details of Wildlife Rescue Centres or in order to receive the BRWC Newsletter write to:

Mr Tim Thomas,
RSPCA Wildlife Department,
Causeway,
Horsham,
West Sussex RH12 1HG

Care for the Wild,
Worldwide Animal Rescue,
1, Ashfolds,
Horsham Road,
Rusper,
West Sussex,
RH12 4QX

(Animal Sponsorship)

Societies

Royal Society for the Prevention of Cruelty to Animals,
Causeway,
Horsham,
West Sussex,
RH12 1HG

(Adult and Child membership)

Royal Society for Nature Conservation,
The Green,
Witham Park,
Lincoln,
LN5 7JR

Somerset Wildlife Trust
Fyne Court,
Broomfield,
Bridgwater,
Somerset,
TA5 2EQ
Tel: 01823 451587

(Child and Adult Membership)

Royal Society for the Protection of Birds,
The Lodge,
Sandy,
Bedfordshire,
SG19 2DL

National Federation of Badger Groups,
15, Cloisters Business Centre,
8, Battersea Park Road,
London,
SW8 4BG

English Nature,
Northminster House,
Peterborough,
Cambridgeshire,
PE1 1UA

Mammal Society,
Cloisters House,
Cloisters Business Centre,
8, Battersea Park Road,
London,
SW8 4BG

The Fox Project,
P.O. Box 56,
Tonbridge,
Kent,
TN9 1XY

The Hedgehog Preservation Society,
Knowbury House,
Ludlow,
Shropshire,
SY8 3LQ

Hedgehog Helpline,
Kay Heaton-Jones,
5, Foreland Road,
Whitchurch,
Cardiff.

Wildlife Courses,
University of Bristol,
Department for Continuing Education,
Wills Memorial Building,
Queens Road,
Bristol,
BS8 1HR

British Chelonian Group,
P.O. Box 235,
Lincoln,
LN6 8AX

Bluebell Sett Wildlife Appeal

We are desperately seeking friends of the farm who will support, through membership of Bluebell Sett, the wildlife work that is carried out at this farm.

Over the years our reputation for taking orphaned and injured animals has grown, many cases being referred to us by vets and the RSPCA as well as members of the public. We have gained experience with all kinds of animals and improved our facilities so that much of the work can be carried out behind the scenes thus aiding recovery by reducing the stress induced by human presence. We have a hospital room with heat lamps, and larger pens to take foxes and badgers that have been injured, usually in road accidents.

Our main aim is to get the animals fit and healthy and then return them to the wild. They are either released where they were found or, if more suitable, from here. Some are taken to the RSPCA Wildlife Unit at Hatch Beauchamp with whom we work very closely.

Over a thousand wild animals have been treated since 1986 when we first started to care for the wild. We never send animals away and are available 24 hours a day – but it is all time-consuming and intensive work. Our vets bill alone is nearly £2000 a year and, like most businesses today we are having to deal with cashflow problems. The bank has now told us that they can no longer support this side of the business which shows no financial return. We feel, however, that the work we do is too important to abandon without trying to raise some support. An annual amount of £5000 is needed.

We are also involved in the National Breeding Programme for the Common Dormouse. Despite the name these delightful creatures are now quite rare and it is hoped to be able to re-introduce them into woodland areas where they have already become extinct.

WOULD YOU LIKE TO JOIN THE BLUEBELL SETT?

Members receive a pack containing a certificate of membership, a car sticker, admission discount vouchers, animal factsheets and a letter from Simon King. The presentation is such that this makes an ideal Christmas or birthday gift. Subscriptions are: adults £12.50, children £7.00; family £30; concessions (OAP and unemployed) £8.50. Please contact Pauline Kidner at Secret World, East Huntspill, Somerset, TA9 3PZ for further details.